Coffee Break: Recharge Your Mind for Peak Performance

AUTHOR

Gerald Carolino

Coffee Break: Recharge Your Mind for Peak Performance

Copyright © 2024 by Gerald S. Carolino All rights reserved. No part of this book may be reproduced or transmitted in any form or by any means without written permission from the author.*ISBN: 9798305344356*

DEDICATION

Coffee Break: Recharge Your Mind for Peak Performance," consider the following dedication: To all the professionals who understand that a simple coffee break can be the catalyst for creativity, productivity, and peak performance.

This book is for you.

Coffee Break: Recharge Your Mind for Peak Performance

"Taking coffee on a busy street in New York

Contents

DEDICATION iii
Acknowledgments i
CHAPTER 1 The Science of Coffee 1
Chapter 2: The Perfect Brew 6
Chapter 3: Timing Your Coffee Breaks 11
Chapter 4: Coffee Rituals for Productivity 16
Chapter 5: Healthy Coffee Habits 21
Chapter 6: Coffee and Creativity 26
Chapter 7: The Future of Coffee in Workspaces 31
Chapter 8: Recap 36
PART-2 41
Coffee Break: Revitalize Your Mind for Success 41
Chapter 1: The Power of a Coffee Break 41
Chapter 2: The Ideal Coffee Break 46
Chapter 3: Mindfulness During Your Break 51
Chapter 4: The Social Aspect of Coffee Breaks 56
Chapter 5: Beyond Coffee: Alternative Breaks 61
Chapter 6: Structuring Your Day for Breaks 66
Chapter 7: Customizing Your Coffee Break Experience 71
Chapter 8: Overcoming Barriers to Taking Breaks 76
Chapter 9: Success Stories: Coffee Breaks in Action 81
Chapter 10: Creating a Coffee Break Plan 86
Author 91

Acknowledgments

Creating "Coffee Break: Recharge Your Mind for Peak Performance" has been a journey fuelled by the support and encouragement of many individuals. A special acknowledgment goes to my sister, Pamela, and my brother-in-law, Rommel, whose visit to their home in New Jersey provided inspiration and motivation. In their household, coffee is the most important drink of the day, keeping us refreshed and energized.

I also wish to express my appreciation to the baristas and coffee enthusiasts who shared their knowledge and passion, providing the foundation for many of the concepts explored in this work.

Lastly, to the readers seeking to enhance their productivity and well-being, this book is for you. May it serve as a catalyst for positive change in your daily life. Thank you all for being part of this journey.

CHAPTER 1 The Science of Coffee

The Origins of Coffee

The history of coffee traces back to ancient Ethiopia, where the stimulating properties of the coffee bean were first discovered. Legend has it that a goat herder named Kaldi observed his goats becoming unusually energetic after eating the red berries from a certain tree. Intrigued, he tried the berries himself and experienced a similar boost in vitality. This discovery led to the spread of coffee as a beverage in the region, eventually making its way to the Arabian Peninsula, where it became an integral part of local culture.

By the 15th century, coffee had established itself in Yemen, with Sufi monks using it to stay awake during long nights of prayer and meditation. The drink gained popularity in the Islamic world, as it provided an alternative to alcohol. Coffeehouses, known as qahveh khaneh, emerged as social hubs for conversation, music, and the exchange of ideas. These establishments became crucial centers for intellectual discourse and played a significant role in the cultural and social fabric of the Middle East.

The 17th century marked the arrival of coffee in Europe, where it quickly captured the attention of the public. The first coffeehouse opened in Venice in 1645, followed by others in major cities like Paris, London, and Vienna. These coffeehouses became known as "penny universities," as patrons could engage in stimulating discussions for the price of a cup of coffee. This new social environment fostered the exchange of ideas and contributed to movements such as the Enlightenment, showcasing coffee's ability to energize not just the body, but also the mind.

As demand for coffee grew, so did the need for production and cultivation. The coffee plant was introduced to various regions around the world, including the Caribbean and South America, where it thrived in the tropical climate. Plantations began to emerge, and coffee became a significant cash crop. The complexities of coffee cultivation and trade would later lead to intricate global networks, shaping economies and societies in the process.

Today, coffee is more than just a beverage; it is a vital part of daily life for millions. Its origins remind us of the rich history and cultural significance behind each cup. Whether it is enjoyed during a break at the office or served in a bustling restaurant, coffee continues to energize and inspire. Understanding the journey of coffee from its humble beginnings to its current status highlights its enduring appeal and importance in our lives, reinforcing the idea that a simple cup can fuel creativity and productivity in our daily routines.

How Coffee Affects the Brain

Coffee is one of the most widely consumed beverages in the world, and its effects on the brain are profound and multifaceted. The primary psychoactive ingredient in coffee is caffeine, a stimulant that affects the central nervous system. Upon consumption, caffeine is quickly absorbed into the bloodstream and travels to the brain, where it blocks the action of adenosine, a neurotransmitter that promotes sleep and relaxation. This blockade leads to increased alertness, improved mood, and enhanced cognitive function, making coffee a popular choice for those seeking to boost their mental performance during demanding tasks.

Research has shown that caffeine can enhance various aspects of cognitive function, including attention, reaction time, and problem-solving abilities. In a restaurant setting, where quick decision-making and multitasking are essential, a cup of coffee can provide the needed mental clarity to navigate a busy environment. Similarly, in an office setting, the stimulating effects of caffeine can help employees stay focused and engaged, particularly during long meetings or challenging projects. This cognitive boost is not only beneficial for individual performance but can also enhance teamwork and collaboration as employees remain alert and responsive.

Moreover, coffee consumption has been linked to long-term cognitive benefits. Studies suggest that regular coffee drinkers may have a lower risk of developing neurodegenerative diseases such as Alzheimer's and Parkinson's. The antioxidants and anti-inflammatory compounds found in coffee may contribute to these protective effects, promoting overall brain health. For those working in high-pressure environments, such as restaurants and offices, maintaining cognitive health is crucial for sustained performance and productivity over time.

While coffee can significantly improve cognitive function, it is essential to consume it in moderation. Excessive intake can lead to negative side effects, including increased anxiety, restlessness, and disrupted sleep patterns. Establishing a healthy relationship with coffee is vital for maximizing its benefits without experiencing adverse effects. For restaurant staff and office workers, understanding personal limits and incorporating strategic coffee breaks can help leverage caffeine's positive effects while maintaining a balanced lifestyle.

Incorporating coffee into daily routines can serve as an effective strategy for enhancing mental performance. For those in the restaurant industry, a well-timed coffee break during a shift can recharge energy levels and sharpen focus, ultimately leading to better service and customer satisfaction. In office environments, coffee breaks can facilitate informal collaboration and idea-sharing, fostering a culture of innovation. By recognizing and harnessing the cognitive benefits of coffee, individuals can power through their day with increased efficiency and effectiveness.

The Role of Caffeine in Performance

Caffeine, a natural stimulant found in coffee, tea, and various energy drinks, plays a significant role in enhancing performance in both cognitive and physical domains. For restaurant staff and office workers, understanding how caffeine influences alertness and productivity can lead to better decision-making regarding its consumption. Studies have shown that caffeine can improve focus, reaction times, and mental clarity, making it an invaluable ally for those in fast-paced environments where efficiency is crucial.

In the context of cognitive performance, caffeine has been shown to enhance attention and concentration. For restaurant employees who must juggle multiple tasks and keep up with the demands of a busy service, a moderate intake of caffeine can help sharpen focus and improve memory retention. This increased mental acuity allows staff to process orders more accurately and respond to customer needs promptly. Similarly, office workers can benefit from caffeine's ability to enhance problem-solving skills and creativity, which are vital for tackling complex projects and collaborating effectively with colleagues.

Additionally, caffeine's impact on physical performance should not be underestimated. For restaurant workers who are often on their feet for long hours, caffeine can serve as a means to combat fatigue and maintain energy levels. Research indicates that caffeine can increase endurance during physical activities, allowing staff to perform at their best without succumbing to exhaustion. For office workers, incorporating caffeine into their routine can provide a much-needed boost during mid-afternoon slumps, helping to sustain energy levels and productivity throughout the day.

However, it is essential to recognize the importance of moderation in caffeine consumption. While it can be a powerful tool for enhancing performance, excessive intake may lead to adverse effects such as jitteriness, anxiety, and disrupted sleep patterns. Restaurant staff and office workers should aim to find a balance that allows them to reap the benefits of caffeine without experiencing negative side effects. Understanding individual tolerance levels and the timing of caffeine consumption can help maximize its positive impacts on performance.

In conclusion, caffeine serves as a valuable resource for enhancing both cognitive and physical performance in restaurant and office settings. By leveraging its benefits, employees can improve focus, increase energy levels, and sustain productivity throughout their demanding workdays. However, it remains crucial to approach caffeine consumption mindfully, ensuring that it supports rather than hinders overall well-being and effectiveness in the workplace.

Chapter 2: The Perfect Brew
Different Brewing Methods

Different brewing methods can significantly impact the flavor, aroma, and overall experience of coffee, making it essential for restaurants and offices to understand the nuances of each technique. Whether aiming to create a memorable coffee experience for customers or providing employees with a quick energy boost, the choice of brewing method can enhance the coffee's qualities. From traditional techniques to modern innovations, each method offers unique benefits and challenges that cater to varying preferences and environments.

The drip brewing method is one of the most widely used techniques, especially in office settings. This method involves pouring hot water over ground coffee in a filter, allowing gravity to extract flavors as the water passes through. Drip coffee makers are convenient, often featuring programmable settings to ensure a fresh brew at any time of the day. For restaurants, drip brewing can produce large quantities of coffee, making it advantageous for catering to busy breakfast or brunch crowds. However, attention to grind size, water temperature, and brew time is crucial to avoid over-extraction or under-extraction, which can lead to undesirable flavors.

French press brewing offers a more hands-on approach that can yield a rich and full-bodied cup of coffee. This method involves steeping coarsely ground coffee in hot water for several minutes before pressing a metal or plastic plunger to separate the grounds from the liquid. The French press allows the essential oils and fine particles to remain in the brew, resulting in a bold flavor profile. This method is ideal for restaurants looking to provide a gourmet coffee experience or for office settings where employees appreciate a more artisanal touch. However, it requires careful monitoring of steeping time to achieve the desired strength.

For those seeking a quick yet flavorful brew, the pour-over method has gained popularity due to its simplicity and ability to highlight coffee's unique characteristics. This technique involves manually pouring hot water over coffee grounds in a filter, allowing for precise control over water flow and extraction time. Pour-over devices, such as the Chemex or Hario V60, can produce a clean and crisp cup, making it a favorite among specialty coffee enthusiasts. In a restaurant setting, pour-over coffee can be a visually appealing option, showcasing the skill of the barista and enhancing the overall dining experience. In offices, it offers a way to engage employees in the coffee-making process, fostering a sense of community.

Lastly, espresso is a brewing method that packs a powerful punch in a small volume. Utilizing high pressure to force hot water through finely ground coffee, espresso produces a concentrated shot that serves as the base for various coffee drinks, including lattes and cappuccinos. This method is particularly valuable in restaurant settings, where the demand for specialty drinks is high. For offices, espresso machines can provide a quick caffeine fix, energizing employees throughout the day. However, mastering the art of espresso extraction requires practice and precision, making it essential to invest in quality equipment and training. Each brewing method brings its unique advantages, allowing restaurants and offices to cater to diverse preferences while maximizing the energizing potential of coffee.

Choosing Quality Coffee Beans

Choosing quality coffee beans is crucial for restaurants and offices aiming to energize their patrons and employees. The journey to exceptional coffee begins with understanding the different types of beans available. The two main varieties are Arabica and Robusta. Arabica beans are known for their smooth, complex flavors and higher acidity, making them a preferred choice for specialty coffee. In contrast, Robusta beans tend to have a stronger, more bitter taste and contain higher caffeine levels, making them suitable for espresso blends. Selecting the right type of bean will significantly influence the overall coffee experience.

When sourcing coffee beans, it's important to consider the origin. The flavor profile of coffee is heavily influenced by where it is grown. Beans from regions like Ethiopia and Colombia offer unique taste notes, ranging from fruity and floral to nutty and chocolaty. Additionally, the altitude at which the coffee is cultivated impacts its quality; higher altitudes generally produce more complex flavors due to slower bean maturation. By understanding these geographical nuances, restaurants and offices can select beans that align with their desired flavor profiles and enhance the coffee experience for their customers and employees.

Freshness is another critical factor to consider when choosing coffee beans. Coffee is best enjoyed within weeks of roasting, as the natural oils responsible for flavor begin to degrade over time. It is advisable for restaurants and offices to establish relationships with local roasters or select suppliers that prioritize fresh, small-batch roasting. This ensures that the beans retain their rich flavors and aromas, providing a satisfying coffee experience that can energize and motivate individuals throughout the day.

Additionally, the quality of coffee beans can be assessed through their processing methods. There are several methods used to process coffee, including washed, natural, and honey processing. Each method affects the final flavor profile of the coffee. For example, natural processing tends to produce a sweeter, fruit-forward flavor, while washed processing highlights the bean's acidity and clarity. Understanding these methods allows restaurants and offices to choose beans that will complement their brewing techniques and meet the preferences of their clientele.

Lastly, sustainability and ethical sourcing should be prioritized when selecting coffee beans. Many consumers today are increasingly concerned about the environmental and social impact of their purchases. By opting for beans that are certified organic, Fair Trade, or Rainforest Alliance, restaurants and offices not only support sustainable farming practices but also enhance their brand image. This commitment to quality and ethical sourcing can resonate with customers and employees alike, fostering a culture of mindfulness and responsibility in the workplace.

Understanding Coffee Strength and Flavor

Coffee strength and flavor are fundamental aspects that can significantly influence the enjoyment and effectiveness of your coffee experience. Understanding these elements is essential for anyone who relies on coffee as a source of energy and focus, especially in restaurant and office settings where productivity is paramount. Coffee strength refers to the concentration of coffee solubles extracted during brewing, while flavor encompasses the complex tastes and aromas that arise from various factors such as bean origin, roast level, and brewing method.

The strength of coffee is typically measured by its caffeine content and the intensity of its flavor. Darker roasts often impart a bolder flavor profile, but they do not necessarily contain more caffeine than lighter roasts. This misconception is rooted in the brewing process and the type of coffee beans used. For instance, a single-origin Ethiopian coffee may have a lighter body but offer vibrant fruity notes that can be perceived as stronger in flavor than a robust dark roast. Understanding this nuance allows coffee drinkers to choose blends that align with their desired flavor profile and energy requirements.

Flavor is influenced by various factors, including the coffee bean's growing conditions, processing methods, and roasting techniques. The terroir, or environmental conditions where the coffee is grown, plays a crucial role in determining the bean's flavor characteristics. For example, beans grown at high altitudes typically develop more complex flavors due to slower maturation. Additionally, the processing method—whether washed, natural, or honey—impacts the final taste. In busy environments like restaurants and offices, selecting the right coffee that reflects these intricate profiles can enhance the overall experience, making each cup a moment of pleasure and rejuvenation.

Brewing methods also significantly affect both the strength and flavor of coffee. Different techniques, such as espresso, pour-over, or French press, yield distinct results. Espresso, known for its concentrated flavor and rich crema, is ideal for those seeking a quick energy boost. In contrast, a pour-over method can highlight the subtleties in flavor, allowing for a more nuanced tasting experience. Understanding these methods empowers individuals to experiment and find the perfect brew that aligns with their personal preferences and energy needs.

Incorporating a deeper understanding of coffee strength and flavor into daily routines can transform coffee consumption into an intentional practice that fuels productivity. For restaurant staff and office workers alike, being mindful of the coffee they choose can lead to increased focus and better performance throughout the day. By appreciating the complexities of coffee, individuals can not only enjoy a richer beverage but also harness its potential to energize their minds and power their days effectively.

Chapter 3: Timing Your Coffee Breaks
The Best Times to Drink Coffee

The timing of coffee consumption can significantly influence its effectiveness as a source of energy and focus. For restaurant workers, early morning shifts often coincide with the need for heightened alertness. Consuming coffee shortly after waking can help jumpstart the day, enhancing cognitive functions and physical stamina. However, it is essential to consider the body's natural circadian rhythm, which typically sees cortisol levels peak shortly after waking. To maximize the energizing effects of caffeine, waiting an hour or so post-wake can ensure that coffee consumption coincides with a natural dip in alertness.

In office settings, mid-morning is often identified as an ideal time for coffee breaks. After a couple of hours of work, employees may experience a slump in energy and concentration. This is when a well-timed coffee break can serve as a powerful productivity booster. Consuming coffee around 9:30 to 11:30 a.m. aligns with the natural post-lunch dip in alertness, providing a necessary lift. It also provides a social aspect, as gathering for coffee can enhance team dynamics and collaboration, making it not just a personal energy boost but a collective one.

For restaurant staff, the lunch rush can be a demanding period. Consuming coffee before the peak hours can help prepare the body and mind for the high-paced environment. However, it is important to avoid caffeine overload, as excessive consumption can lead to jitteriness and decreased performance. A balanced approach, perhaps a smaller cup or a lighter brew, can help maintain energy without overwhelming the senses. This strategic timing ensures that coffee serves as a reliable ally in navigating the challenges of busy service periods.

In the afternoon, the "post-lunch dip" is a common experience in both restaurants and offices. This is often when energy levels drop, and focus wanes. A well-timed afternoon coffee can help counteract this lull. Research suggests that consuming caffeine around 2:00 to 3:00 p.m. can effectively re-energize individuals, improving alertness and cognitive function for the remainder of the day. It allows for a refreshing break, which can also serve as a mental reset, fostering creativity and problem-solving skills.

Finally, it's worth noting that individual preferences and tolerances to caffeine vary widely. Some individuals may find that late-afternoon coffee disrupts their sleep patterns, while others may thrive on it. Personal experimentation with timing can lead to optimal results. Additionally, hydration and nutrition play crucial roles in how coffee impacts energy levels. By strategically planning coffee breaks throughout the day, both restaurant and office workers can harness the full potential of coffee as a tool for mental and physical performance.

Coffee and Circadian Rhythms

Coffee consumption has been a staple in many workplaces and restaurants, often serving as a necessary fuel for long hours and demanding tasks. However, its impact on our circadian rhythms—our internal biological clock regulating sleep and wakefulness—can be both beneficial and detrimental. Understanding how coffee interacts with these rhythms is essential for optimizing productivity and maintaining overall well-being in environments where energy and focus are paramount.

Circadian rhythms are influenced by a variety of factors, with light exposure being one of the most significant. These rhythms dictate the release of hormones like melatonin and cortisol, which in turn affect our alertness and energy levels throughout the day. Coffee, primarily due to its caffeine content, plays a crucial role in this dynamic. When consumed strategically, it can enhance alertness during peak hours of productivity, helping individuals stay focused and energized. However, excessive consumption, especially later in the day, can disrupt sleep patterns, leading to a cycle of fatigue and reliance on caffeine.

Research indicates that the timing of coffee consumption is critical for aligning with natural circadian rhythms. Consuming coffee shortly after waking can enhance cognitive functions and improve mood, as cortisol levels are naturally higher in the morning. This peak in cortisol, coupled with caffeine, can lead to heightened alertness and performance. As the day progresses, however, the timing of caffeine intake becomes more crucial. Consuming coffee too late can interfere with the body's ability to wind down, leading to difficulties in falling asleep and ultimately affecting the next day's performance.

For both restaurant and office environments, understanding the relationship between coffee and circadian rhythms can inform policies around coffee breaks and consumption practices. Encouraging employees to consume coffee during the mid-morning slump or early afternoon can help maximize its benefits while minimizing negative effects on sleep. Establishing designated coffee breaks can also foster a culture of mindfulness, allowing individuals to recharge not only with caffeine but also through social interaction and brief periods of rest.

Ultimately, the key to harnessing the power of coffee while respecting circadian rhythms lies in moderation and timing. By strategically integrating coffee into daily routines, both office workers and restaurant staff can enhance their cognitive performance and energy levels, leading to greater productivity and job satisfaction. Understanding these rhythms allows individuals to use coffee not just as a pick-me-up, but as a tool for achieving peak performance throughout the day.

Avoiding the Afternoon Slump

Coffee Break: Recharge Your Mind for Peak Performance

The afternoon slump is a common challenge faced by many professionals in restaurants and offices alike. As the clock ticks past lunch, energy levels often dip, resulting in decreased productivity and focus. Understanding the physiological and psychological factors contributing to this phenomenon can help individuals develop strategies to combat it effectively. Factors such as post-lunch fatigue, circadian rhythms, and the natural ebb and flow of energy throughout the day play significant roles in this mid-afternoon dip.

One of the most effective ways to avoid the afternoon slump is to pay attention to nutrition. A heavy lunch, particularly one high in carbohydrates, can lead to a quick spike in blood sugar followed by a crash. Opting for lighter meals that include a balance of protein, healthy fats, and complex carbohydrates can help maintain steady energy levels. Incorporating foods rich in vitamins and minerals, such as leafy greens and whole grains, can also provide sustained energy without the subsequent crash often associated with less healthy choices.

In addition to mindful eating, staying hydrated is crucial in preventing fatigue. Dehydration can exacerbate feelings of tiredness and hinder cognitive function. Encouraging regular water intake throughout the day can help keep energy levels stable. For those who enjoy coffee, timing is everything; strategically consuming caffeine in moderation can offer a boost without leading to jitters or a crash later. A mid-afternoon cup of coffee can be particularly effective when paired with a light snack to enhance focus and alertness.

Movement is another powerful tool in combating the afternoon slump. Incorporating short breaks for physical activity can invigorate both the mind and body. Simple activities such as stretching, walking, or even brief exercises can increase circulation and release endorphins, which improve mood and energy levels. Restaurants and offices can benefit from creating an environment that encourages movement, such as designated break areas or promoting walking meetings. These small changes can make a significant difference in maintaining productivity throughout the day.

Finally, addressing mental fatigue is essential in avoiding the afternoon slump. Engaging in activities that stimulate the mind, such as brainstorming sessions or collaborative tasks, can help break the monotony of routine and reinvigorate focus. Implementing techniques like mindfulness or brief meditation can also aid in re-centering thoughts and enhancing clarity. By creating a culture that values breaks and recognizes the importance of mental wellness, both restaurant and office environments can foster sustained energy and productivity, ensuring that the afternoon slump becomes a thing of the past.

Chapter 4: Coffee Rituals for Productivity

Creating a Coffee Break Routine

Creating a coffee break routine is essential for maximizing productivity and enhancing mental clarity in both restaurant and office environments. A well-structured coffee break can serve as a vital recharge point throughout the day, helping employees to reset their focus and creativity. The key is to design a routine that not only incorporates the enjoyment of coffee but also includes activities that foster relaxation and social interaction, ultimately leading to improved performance.

To begin, establish a designated time for coffee breaks. Consistency is important; setting specific intervals during the workday—such as mid-morning and mid-afternoon—helps in creating a habit. This predictability allows employees to anticipate their breaks, making them more effective in managing their time and workload. In restaurant settings, managers can coordinate breaks among staff to ensure that customer service remains uninterrupted while still providing employees with the downtime they need to recharge.

Next, consider the environment in which coffee breaks take place. A comfortable and inviting space can significantly enhance the quality of the break. In office settings, this could mean creating a cozy break room with comfortable seating and adequate lighting. For restaurants, a designated staff room or outdoor patio can serve as a refreshing escape from the fast-paced environment of the dining area. Incorporating elements of nature, such as plants or natural light, can further promote relaxation and rejuvenation.

In addition to enjoying coffee, encourage employees to engage in activities that promote mental relaxation and social interaction during their breaks. Simple options include light conversation with coworkers, sharing personal experiences, or discussing non-work-related topics. Additionally, incorporating mindfulness practices, such as deep breathing or stretching, can help clear the mind and reduce stress. Providing access to reading materials or puzzles can also stimulate the brain in a low-pressure setting, allowing for a refreshing mental shift.

Lastly, gather feedback from employees on the coffee break routine to ensure it remains effective and enjoyable. Regularly assess what aspects are working well and what could be improved. This feedback loop not only helps in refining the routine but also fosters a sense of ownership among employees. By recognizing the importance of coffee breaks and actively involving staff in the process, both restaurant and office environments can cultivate a culture that prioritizes mental well-being, ultimately leading to enhanced performance and job satisfaction.

Mindfulness During Coffee Breaks

Mindfulness during coffee breaks can significantly enhance the benefits of this common ritual in both restaurant and office environments. The act of pausing to enjoy coffee offers an opportunity to step away from the hustle and bustle, allowing individuals to recharge both mentally and physically. By incorporating mindfulness into this routine, employees can cultivate a greater sense of awareness and presence, which can lead to improved focus, clarity, and overall well-being.

To practice mindfulness during coffee breaks, start by creating a dedicated space and time for your break. This can be a quiet corner in the office or a cozy spot in the restaurant. As you prepare your coffee, take a moment to appreciate the aroma and the warmth of the cup in your hands. Engage your senses fully—notice the colors, textures, and sounds around you. This deliberate attention to your surroundings helps anchor your mind in the

present moment, making it easier to let go of stress and distractions.
Once seated, take a few deep breaths before sipping your coffee. Allow yourself to savor each sip, noticing the flavor and the sensations it brings. This practice of mindful drinking can transform a simple coffee break into a sensory experience that grounds you. Rather than consuming your beverage mindlessly while multitasking, focus solely on the act of drinking. This shift in attention can enhance your appreciation for the coffee, making it a more rewarding experience.

In a bustling work environment, it may be tempting to check emails or scroll through social media during your break. However, resisting this urge is crucial for cultivating mindfulness. Instead, consider disconnecting from technology for a few minutes. Use this time to reflect on your thoughts or simply observe the world around you. This practice not only fosters a sense of calm but also encourages creativity, allowing fresh ideas to surface when you return to your tasks.

Incorporating mindfulness into coffee breaks can lead to long-term benefits for both individuals and teams. Improved focus and reduced stress levels can enhance productivity and overall job satisfaction. Additionally, when employees take the time to recharge mindfully, they are more likely to return to their work with renewed energy and motivation. By embracing mindfulness during these short breaks, you can create a culture of well-being that fosters peak performance in the restaurant and office settings.

Socializing Over Coffee: Building Team Spirit

Socializing over coffee serves as a powerful tool for building team spirit in both restaurant and office settings. The act of gathering around a coffee machine or a cozy café table fosters a relaxed atmosphere that encourages open dialogue and connection among team members. This informal environment can break down barriers that often exist in more formal settings, allowing individuals to engage in meaningful conversations that strengthen relationships and promote collaboration. As teams bond over their shared love of coffee, they also enhance their ability to work together effectively, which ultimately benefits the workplace culture.

In addition to facilitating communication, coffee breaks provide a much-needed pause in the day, allowing employees to recharge. The caffeine in coffee can boost alertness and energy levels, enabling team members to return to their tasks with renewed focus and enthusiasm. By scheduling regular coffee breaks, organizations can create a rhythm in the workday that not only enhances productivity but also reinforces a sense of community among staff. This practice can be particularly beneficial in high-pressure environments like restaurants, where teamwork is essential for delivering exceptional customer service.

Moreover, coffee breaks can serve as an opportunity for team bonding through shared experiences. Teams can use this time to celebrate successes, brainstorm ideas, or even discuss challenges in a supportive setting. By encouraging team members to share their thoughts and suggestions over coffee, organizations can foster an inclusive culture where everyone feels valued and heard. This collaborative spirit can lead to innovative solutions and improved morale, as employees feel more connected to both their colleagues and the organization's goals.

The social aspect of coffee breaks also plays a critical role in enhancing employee well-being. Taking time to step away from work and engage in casual conversations can reduce stress and improve overall job satisfaction. In fast-paced environments, it's easy for employees to become overwhelmed, but a short coffee break can provide a mental reset. When employees feel supported and connected, they are more likely to exhibit higher levels of engagement and commitment to their work, which is vital for retention and performance.

Lastly, incorporating coffee breaks into the workplace culture can signify a commitment to employee wellness. Organizations that prioritize these moments of socialization demonstrate an understanding of the importance of work-life balance. By creating designated times for employees to come together, share ideas, and enjoy a cup of coffee, companies can cultivate a positive atmosphere that enhances teamwork. In the long run, this not only improves individual performance but also contributes to the overall success of the organization.

Chapter 5: Healthy Coffee Habits
Balancing Coffee with Hydration

Coffee is often celebrated for its stimulating effects, providing an energy boost that many people rely on throughout their busy days in restaurants and offices. However, the consumption of coffee can lead to a potential imbalance in hydration levels, particularly because caffeine acts as a mild diuretic. Understanding how to balance coffee intake with proper hydration is essential for maintaining optimal performance and well-being, allowing individuals to enjoy their coffee without compromising their health.

The first step in balancing coffee with hydration is to be mindful of the amount of coffee consumed daily. While moderate coffee intake can be beneficial, excessive consumption may lead to dehydration. It is generally recommended to limit coffee intake to about three to four cups per day, depending on individual tolerance and lifestyle. This moderation helps maintain hydration levels while still enjoying the cognitive and physical benefits that coffee provides. Pairing coffee with water or other hydrating beverages throughout the day can help offset the dehydrating effects of caffeine.

Incorporating water breaks into the daily routine can enhance hydration without sacrificing the enjoyment of coffee. For every cup of coffee consumed, it is advisable to drink an equal amount of water. This practice not only helps counterbalance the potential diuretic effects of caffeine but also keeps the body refreshed and energized. Establishing a habit of alternating between coffee and water can create a sustainable approach to hydration, ensuring that individuals remain alert and focused throughout their workday. Additionally, considering the timing of coffee consumption can play a significant role in hydration balance. Drinking coffee first thing in the morning may lead to an early onset of dehydration, especially if it replaces a glass of water. Starting the day with a glass of water before enjoying coffee can help kickstart hydration. Similarly, avoiding coffee in the late afternoon or evening can prevent sleep disturbances, allowing for better recovery and hydration overnight. Timing is key to maximizing the benefits of coffee while maintaining adequate hydration.

Finally, paying attention to the body's signals is crucial. Signs of dehydration, such as dry mouth, fatigue, and headaches, can often be mistaken for the need for another cup of coffee. By recognizing these cues and responding with water intake instead, individuals can foster a healthier relationship with caffeine. Emphasizing hydration alongside coffee consumption will not only enhance cognitive function and energy levels but also contribute to overall well-being, allowing restaurant staff and office workers to perform at their peak throughout the day.

Recognizing Caffeine Sensitivity

Caffeine sensitivity varies significantly among individuals, impacting how one experiences the effects of coffee. Recognizing whether you fall into the category of caffeine-sensitive individuals can greatly influence your coffee consumption habits and overall productivity. Caffeine sensitivity is often determined by genetic factors, which affect how quickly caffeine is metabolized in the body. Those with a slower metabolism may experience heightened effects from smaller amounts of caffeine, leading to anxiety, restlessness, or sleep disturbances.

The first sign of caffeine sensitivity is often an exaggerated response to its consumption. For instance, while some individuals may enjoy a cup of coffee to boost alertness, caffeine-sensitive individuals might feel jittery or anxious after just one cup. Monitoring your body's reaction after consuming caffeine can help you identify your sensitivity level. Noticing how your heart rate, mood, or sleep patterns change after coffee intake can provide valuable insights. If you experience negative side effects even with moderate consumption, it may be time to reassess your caffeine habits.

Another important factor to consider is tolerance. Over time, regular caffeine consumers may develop a tolerance, meaning they require larger amounts to achieve the same energizing effects. Conversely, caffeine-sensitive individuals may not build tolerance as quickly, resulting in a consistent reaction to caffeine intake. This dynamic can complicate the relationship with coffee, especially in environments like restaurants and offices where coffee is frequently available. Understanding this distinction can help individuals make informed choices about their caffeine consumption to maintain energy without negative repercussions.

To further gauge caffeine sensitivity, consider keeping a diary of your coffee consumption and its effects on your daily performance. Note the times you drink coffee, the amount consumed, and how you feel afterward. This can reveal patterns that indicate your personal threshold for caffeine. In high-paced environments, such as restaurants or offices, being aware of how caffeine affects your focus and stress levels can lead to better decision-making regarding when and how much coffee to consume.

Ultimately, recognizing caffeine sensitivity is essential for optimizing mental performance and well-being. By understanding your body's unique response to caffeine, you can tailor your coffee intake to enhance productivity without the adverse effects. This knowledge empowers you to make strategic choices that align with your energy needs, enabling you to recharge effectively and maintain peak performance throughout the day.

Alternatives to Traditional Coffee

As the demand for coffee continues to rise, many individuals and businesses are exploring alternatives that can provide similar energizing effects without

Coffee Break: Recharge Your Mind for Peak Performance

relying solely on traditional coffee. These alternatives not only cater to diverse tastes and dietary preferences but also offer unique health benefits. Understanding these options can help restaurants and offices create a more inclusive beverage menu that supports peak performance and mental clarity. One popular alternative gaining traction is matcha, a finely ground powder made from specially grown green tea leaves. Unlike regular green tea, matcha involves consuming the whole leaf, which maximizes the intake of antioxidants and nutrients. Matcha contains L-theanine, an amino acid that promotes relaxation without drowsiness, making it an ideal choice for maintaining focus during long meetings or busy shifts. Additionally, the caffeine content in matcha provides a gentler energy boost compared to coffee, reducing the risk of jitters and crashes.

Herbal teas are another excellent substitute for traditional coffee, offering a wide range of flavors and health benefits. Varieties such as rooibos, chamomile, and peppermint not only hydrate the body but also provide unique properties. For instance, rooibos is caffeine-free and rich in antioxidants, making it suitable for evening consumption while promoting relaxation. Incorporating herbal teas into a beverage menu can appeal to those looking for a calming experience after a hectic day or a refreshing option during breaks.

Yerba mate, a traditional South American drink, is also garnering attention as a coffee alternative. Known for its rich caffeine content, yerba mate provides a smooth energy boost accompanied by a distinct flavor profile. It is also rich in vitamins and minerals, contributing to overall health. Offering yerba mate in restaurants or offices can introduce a cultural experience while catering to those who prefer a different taste than coffee but still seek the stimulating effects of caffeine.

Finally, plant-based energy drinks have emerged as a modern alternative to traditional coffee. These beverages often combine natural ingredients like guarana, ginseng, and various fruit extracts to provide energy without the acidity associated with coffee. Many of these drinks are formulated to enhance mental clarity and endurance, making them suitable for both busy office environments and dynamic restaurant settings. By incorporating these alternatives, establishments can not only diversify their beverage offerings but also promote a culture of health and wellness among their patrons and staff.

Chapter 6: Coffee and Creativity
Stimulating Creative Thinking

Stimulating creative thinking is essential for professionals in both the restaurant and office environments, where innovative ideas can lead to improved processes and enhanced customer experiences. Creativity is not merely an innate trait; it can be cultivated through various strategies and practices. One effective method is to create an environment that encourages free thinking and open dialogue. This can be achieved by arranging spaces that invite collaboration, ensuring that team members feel comfortable sharing their ideas without fear of judgment. Simple changes, such as incorporating communal areas for brainstorming or using visual aids like whiteboards and sticky notes, can significantly enhance the creative output of teams.

Another important aspect of stimulating creativity is the role of coffee as a cognitive enhancer. The caffeine in coffee can improve alertness and focus, which are critical for generating new ideas. When consumed in moderation, coffee can increase the brain's capacity to process information and foster connections between seemingly unrelated concepts. This heightened mental state can be particularly beneficial during brainstorming sessions, where the objective is to generate as many ideas as possible. Creating a coffee culture within the workplace, where breaks are encouraged and coffee is readily available, can help establish a routine that fosters creativity.

In addition to the physical environment and coffee consumption, engaging in activities that promote divergent thinking is crucial. Techniques such as mind mapping, role-playing, and lateral thinking exercises can help individuals and teams explore different perspectives and challenge conventional assumptions. These activities not only stimulate creative thought but also encourage participants to step outside their comfort zones, which is often where the most innovative ideas emerge. Regularly incorporating such exercises into team meetings can lead to a more dynamic and open-minded work culture. Collaboration is another key element in fostering creative thinking. Working with diverse teams brings together a wealth of experiences and viewpoints, which can lead to more innovative solutions. Encouraging cross-departmental projects or hosting collaborative workshops can help break down silos and promote a culture of shared creativity. In the restaurant setting, this could involve chefs working with front-of-house staff to create new menu items that resonate with customers, while in an office environment, different departments can team up to solve common challenges.

Lastly, it is essential to recognize and celebrate creativity within the workplace. Acknowledging and rewarding innovative ideas not only boosts morale but also encourages continued creative efforts. Implementing recognition programs that highlight successful projects or unique contributions can motivate employees to think creatively and share their ideas freely. By fostering an environment that values creativity and innovation, both restaurants and offices can enhance their overall performance and maintain a competitive edge in their respective markets.

Case Studies: Coffee and Successful Innovators

Case studies of successful innovators in the coffee industry reveal how creativity and strategic thinking can transform a simple beverage into a powerful business model. One notable example is Starbucks, which revolutionized the coffee shop experience by focusing on creating a third place between home and work. By emphasizing ambiance, customer experience, and quality, Starbucks not only popularized specialty coffee but also created a global community around it. This innovative approach has led to the company's remarkable growth, demonstrating how a strong brand identity coupled with consumer-centric strategies can lead to success. Another compelling case is that of Blue Bottle Coffee, a company that emerged from the artisanal coffee movement. Founded in 2002, Blue Bottle prioritized freshness and quality, sourcing beans from small farms and roasting them in small batches. Its philosophy of "less is more" resonated with a growing demographic of coffee enthusiasts who valued transparency and sustainability. By creating a niche market focused on high-quality coffee, Blue Bottle was able to carve out a unique position in a crowded marketplace, attracting both casual drinkers and connoisseurs alike.

Additionally, the rise of cold brew coffee can be attributed to innovators such as Stumptown Coffee Roasters. This company not only popularized cold brew but also set standards for quality and flavor. Stumptown's attention to detail in sourcing beans and its commitment to direct trade relationships with farmers highlighted the importance of ethical practices in the coffee supply chain. This focus on quality and ethics has resonated with consumers, leading to a loyal customer base and an expansion of its product offerings, including ready-to-drink cold brews.

In the realm of technology, companies like Brewed Awakening have utilized mobile apps and subscription services to enhance the coffee experience. By integrating technology into the coffee-buying process, they have streamlined ordering and payment, making it more convenient for consumers. This innovative approach has not only improved customer satisfaction but also provided valuable data analytics that inform business decisions and marketing strategies. The intersection of technology and coffee demonstrates how embracing innovation can lead to enhanced operational efficiency and customer engagement.

These case studies illustrate that successful innovators in the coffee industry share common traits such as a deep understanding of consumer preferences, a commitment to quality, and a willingness to adapt to changing market dynamics. By analyzing these strategies, restaurant and office professionals can glean valuable insights on how to harness the energizing potential of coffee to enhance workplace performance and foster a vibrant culture around this beloved beverage. The stories of these innovators serve as a reminder that creativity and strategic thinking are essential components in transforming an ordinary product into an extraordinary experience.

Activities to Enhance Creativity with Coffee

Activities to enhance creativity with coffee can significantly benefit both restaurant staff and office workers. The unique properties of coffee, particularly its caffeine content, stimulate the brain and can lead to improved focus and creativity. Incorporating specific activities into coffee breaks can help tap into this potential, transforming a simple coffee break into a powerful tool for innovation and problem-solving.

One effective activity is brainstorming sessions held during coffee breaks. This informal setting encourages participants to share ideas freely without the pressure of a formal meeting. The relaxed atmosphere, combined with the stimulating effects of coffee, can lead to more creative thinking and the generation of innovative solutions. To maximize the effectiveness of these sessions, set a clear topic or challenge to focus discussions, and allow for open-ended contributions from all team members.

Another engaging way to harness creativity is through collaborative coffee art or design challenges. Participants can take a few moments to create latte art or design a new coffee blend using available ingredients. This hands-on activity not only fosters teamwork but also engages the mind in a creative process. Sharing the results can spark conversations and lead to new ideas for menu items or marketing strategies, enhancing the overall coffee experience for customers.

Incorporating movement into coffee breaks can also boost creativity. Simple stretching or light exercises can invigorate the mind and body, making individuals more receptive to new ideas. For restaurants, a brief walk around the dining area or kitchen can inspire fresh perspectives on service or menu presentation. In office settings, walking meetings with coffee in hand can stimulate brainstorming and foster a dynamic exchange of ideas, further enhancing creativity.

Finally, setting up a coffee and idea exchange wall can facilitate ongoing creativity. Team members can post their thoughts, suggestions, or questions related to coffee, work processes, or menu innovations. This visual and interactive approach encourages collaboration and continuous idea flow, making creativity a regular part of the workplace culture. By integrating these activities into coffee breaks, restaurants and offices can turn a daily ritual into a catalyst for enhanced creativity and performance.

Chapter 7: The Future of Coffee in Workspaces

Trends in Office Coffee Culture

The evolution of office coffee culture has significantly transformed the way employees interact, recharge, and enhance their productivity. Traditionally, coffee was merely a functional beverage consumed to stave off fatigue during long work hours. However, the modern office environment has embraced coffee as a vital component of workplace culture, cultivating an atmosphere that fosters collaboration, creativity, and wellness. Organizations now recognize that high-quality coffee options can contribute to a more engaged workforce, leading to a shift from the basic coffee maker to a diverse array of brewing methods and specialty coffee offerings.

One prominent trend in office coffee culture is the increasing preference for specialty coffee. Employees are becoming more discerning about their coffee choices, seeking out premium beans and artisanal brews. This shift has prompted companies to invest in high-quality coffee machines, bean subscriptions, and training for staff to prepare coffee that meets the rising expectations of their workforce. By providing access to specialty coffee, employers not only enhance the coffee experience but also demonstrate a commitment to employee satisfaction and well-being.

Another significant trend is the incorporation of sustainability into coffee sourcing practices. As awareness of environmental issues grows, many companies are opting for ethically sourced and organic coffee. This trend reflects a broader commitment to corporate social responsibility and aligns with the values of a workforce that increasingly prioritizes sustainability. By choosing coffee suppliers that practice fair trade and sustainable farming, organizations can reduce their environmental footprint while also fostering a sense of purpose among employees who appreciate the impact of their choices.

The social aspect of coffee consumption in the workplace is also evolving. Coffee breaks are no longer seen as mere pauses in productivity; they are now opportunities for team bonding and informal collaboration. Open office designs often feature communal coffee stations that encourage employees to gather and engage with one another. This shift not only enhances interpersonal relationships but also cultivates a sense of community, which can lead to improved morale and job satisfaction. As a result, coffee has become a catalyst for creating a more connected and productive workplace.

Lastly, the rise of remote and hybrid work models has influenced office coffee culture in unique ways. With employees working from various locations, including home, many organizations are exploring ways to replicate the coffee culture experience outside the traditional office. This may include providing coffee subscriptions for remote workers or hosting virtual coffee breaks to maintain connections. By adapting to the changing landscape of work, companies can ensure that coffee remains a central part of their culture, helping to energize their teams and keep morale high in any setting.

Sustainable Coffee Practices

Sustainable coffee practices are essential for ensuring that the coffee industry can thrive without compromising the environment or the livelihoods of those involved in its production. The journey of coffee from farm to cup is often fraught with ecological challenges, including deforestation, water pollution, and the exploitation of labor. By adopting sustainable practices, restaurants and offices can make a positive impact, contributing to a more responsible coffee supply chain. This not only helps protect the planet but also enhances the quality of the coffee served, ultimately benefiting the consumer.

One of the key components of sustainable coffee practices is the cultivation of coffee beans using environmentally friendly methods. Shade-grown coffee is one such approach, where coffee plants are grown under the canopy of trees. This method promotes biodiversity, protects soil quality, and conserves water resources. Additionally, it provides habitat for various wildlife species. When restaurants and offices prioritize shade-grown coffee, they support farmers who are committed to these sustainable practices, fostering a more resilient agricultural ecosystem.

Another important aspect is the certification of coffee through various sustainable programs. Look for labels such as Fair Trade, Rainforest Alliance, or organic certifications. These labels indicate that the coffee has been produced under ethical conditions that prioritize fair wages for farmers, environmentally friendly practices, and community development. By sourcing certified coffee, restaurants and offices can assure their customers that their beverage choices contribute to positive social and environmental outcomes, creating a more conscientious consumer experience.

Waste management is also a significant component of sustainable coffee practices. In many establishments, coffee grounds and other byproducts can be repurposed rather than discarded. For example, coffee grounds can be composted to enrich soil, used as a natural pest repellent, or even incorporated into scrubs and soaps. Additionally, restaurants can explore options for recycling coffee packaging and utilizing energy-efficient brewing equipment. This holistic approach to waste management not only minimizes environmental impact but also enhances the overall sustainability of coffee offerings.

Finally, educating staff and consumers about sustainable coffee practices can foster a culture of sustainability within restaurants and offices. Providing information on the origins of the coffee served, the importance of sustainable sourcing, and the environmental impact of coffee production can empower customers to make informed choices. Engaging in local community efforts, such as hosting coffee tastings or collaborating with sustainable coffee producers, can further promote awareness and appreciation for sustainable coffee. By integrating these practices into everyday operations, restaurants and offices can ensure that their coffee breaks are not only energizing but also aligned with a vision for a more sustainable future.

The Role of Coffee in Employee Wellness Programs

Coffee has become an integral part of the daily routine for many employees in both restaurant and office settings. Its popularity extends beyond mere enjoyment; coffee serves as a vital component in employee wellness programs aimed at enhancing productivity and overall well-being. By incorporating coffee into these programs, organizations can create an environment that not only fosters energy and focus but also promotes social interaction and collaboration among employees.

Research indicates that moderate coffee consumption can improve cognitive function, increase alertness, and enhance mood. This is particularly relevant in high-paced environments like restaurants and offices, where employees often face demanding workloads. Offering coffee as part of wellness initiatives can help mitigate fatigue and maintain high levels of engagement throughout the day. Providing access to quality coffee can lead to a more invigorated workforce, ultimately benefiting the organization's bottom line through improved performance and efficiency.

Moreover, coffee can serve as a catalyst for social interaction, which is a crucial aspect of employee wellness. Breaks that include coffee consumption can facilitate informal conversations and networking among colleagues, promoting a sense of community within the workplace. This social engagement helps to reduce feelings of isolation and stress, contributing positively to mental health. Thus, coffee breaks can transform into valuable opportunities for team building and collaboration, enhancing workplace culture.

Incorporating coffee into wellness programs can also align with broader health initiatives. Many organizations are recognizing the importance of hydration and balanced nutrition as part of their wellness strategies. By offering coffee alongside healthy snacks and water stations, companies can encourage employees to make better choices throughout the day. Additionally, educational workshops about the benefits of coffee, such as its antioxidants and potential health advantages, can empower employees to appreciate coffee as a functional beverage rather than just a daily ritual.

Finally, it is essential for organizations to be mindful of how coffee is presented in the workplace. Providing high-quality coffee options, including specialty blends and fair-trade choices, can enhance the overall experience for employees. Moreover, creating comfortable spaces for coffee breaks can encourage employees to take the time they need to recharge. By thoughtfully integrating coffee into employee wellness programs, organizations can foster an environment that not only promotes productivity but also prioritizes the health and happiness of their workforce.

Coffee Break: Recharge Your Mind for Peak Performance

Chapter 8: Recap

Recap of Key Concepts

In the pursuit of peak performance, understanding the fundamental concepts surrounding coffee and its impact on our cognitive functions is essential. Coffee, a beloved beverage in both restaurant and office settings, serves as more than just a morning ritual; it is a powerful tool for enhancing mental clarity and productivity. The primary ingredient, caffeine, stimulates the central nervous system, leading to increased alertness and reduced perception of fatigue. This makes coffee an ideal companion during long hours of work or busy shifts, helping individuals maintain focus and energy levels.

One of the key concepts discussed in this book is the importance of timing when consuming coffee. To maximize its benefits, it is crucial to align coffee consumption with the body's natural circadian rhythms. The optimal times for coffee intake generally fall between mid-morning and early afternoon, as this aligns with the body's natural dip in energy levels. By strategically timing coffee breaks, individuals can not only enhance their performance but also avoid the negative effects of caffeine, such as jitteriness or disrupted sleep patterns later in the day.

Another significant aspect covered is the role of coffee in enhancing cognitive functions. Studies have shown that moderate coffee consumption can improve memory, attention, and overall cognitive performance. For those working in fast-paced environments like restaurants or offices, these enhanced cognitive abilities can lead to better decision making, quicker problem-solving, and improved interpersonal communication. Understanding how coffee affects the brain empowers individuals to use it effectively as a performance enhancer rather than simply a source of temporary energy.

The social aspect of coffee consumption is also noteworthy. Coffee breaks serve as a crucial opportunity for team bonding and collaboration in both restaurants and offices. These breaks not only provide a moment to recharge but also facilitate informal discussions that can lead to innovative ideas and solutions. Recognizing the value of these interactions can enhance workplace culture and productivity, making coffee breaks a vital component of both personal and team success.

Lastly, it is essential to acknowledge the variety of coffee options available and their differing effects. From espresso shots to cold brews, each type of coffee offers unique benefits and flavor profiles. Understanding these differences allows individuals to select the right coffee for their specific needs and preferences. By becoming more informed about coffee, individuals can tailor their consumption habits to best support their mental performance and overall well-being, ultimately leading to greater success in their professional and personal lives.

Implementing Coffee Break Strategies

Implementing coffee break strategies in both restaurant and office settings can significantly enhance productivity and employee well-being. The concept of a coffee break is not merely a pause in the workday; it is an opportunity to recharge, refocus, and reinvigorate the mind. By establishing structured coffee break strategies, businesses can create an environment that fosters creativity and collaboration while also ensuring employees feel valued and refreshed.

One effective strategy is to schedule regular coffee breaks throughout the day. In a restaurant setting, this could mean allowing staff to take short breaks between shifts or during less busy times. For office environments, creating designated break times can help employees step away from their desks and disconnect from their tasks. These scheduled breaks should be communicated clearly to all staff, encouraging them to take full advantage of the time allotted for relaxation and socializing.

Another important aspect of implementing coffee break strategies is to create a dedicated space for these breaks. A comfortable and inviting area where employees can enjoy their coffee, engage in conversation, or simply relax can make a significant difference in the overall break experience. For restaurants, this could be a cozy staff lounge, while in offices, a well-designed break room or outdoor space can serve the same purpose. The ambiance of the coffee break area should promote relaxation and encourage informal interactions among employees.

Incorporating coffee-related activities into break times can also enhance the experience. For example, hosting regular coffee tastings or workshops can provide employees with a deeper appreciation for their beverage and foster team bonding. In an office setting, this could involve inviting local roasters to share insights about coffee brewing or offering barista training sessions. Such activities not only make the coffee break more engaging but also promote a culture of learning and exploration within the workplace.

Finally, it is essential to encourage a culture that values breaks as a necessary part of the workday. Management should lead by example, taking breaks themselves and demonstrating the importance of stepping away from work to recharge. By promoting a positive attitude toward coffee breaks, businesses can ensure that employees feel empowered to take the time they need, ultimately leading to improved focus, creativity, and overall performance. Implementing these strategies can transform coffee breaks into powerful tools for enhancing workplace dynamics and productivity.

Final Thoughts on Coffee and Performance

Coffee has long been a staple in both restaurant and office environments, serving as a quick energizer and a social lubricant. Its rich history and cultural significance have turned it into more than just a beverage; for many, it is an essential component of their daily routine. Understanding the impact of coffee on performance can help individuals and businesses harness its potential to foster productivity, creativity, and enhanced mental clarity.

The caffeine in coffee is known for its ability to stimulate the central nervous system. This stimulation results in increased alertness and reduced perception of fatigue, which can be particularly beneficial in high-pressure environments like restaurants and offices. For employees facing long hours or demanding tasks, a strategic coffee break can provide a much-needed boost. The timing of coffee consumption plays a crucial role, as consuming coffee during natural dips in energy can maximize its effects, helping to sustain high levels of performance throughout the day.

Moreover, coffee consumption is associated with a variety of cognitive benefits. Studies have shown that moderate coffee intake can improve mood, enhance concentration, and sharpen focus. These effects can lead to improved teamwork and collaboration in an office setting, as well as quicker reaction times and better decision-making in a fast-paced restaurant environment. By encouraging mindful coffee breaks, employers can foster a culture that prioritizes mental well-being and peak performance among their teams.

However, it is essential to approach coffee consumption with a balanced mindset. Over-reliance on caffeine can lead to negative side effects, including anxiety, jitters, and disruptions in sleep patterns. Establishing clear guidelines around coffee breaks can prevent excessive consumption and encourage a healthy relationship with caffeine. By promoting awareness of individual tolerance levels and providing alternatives such as herbal teas or decaffeinated options, organizations can support their employees in maintaining optimal performance without the pitfalls associated with overconsumption.

In conclusion, coffee continues to be an incredibly potent and versatile tool for enhancing performance across a wide range of environments, including both bustling restaurant settings and dynamic office spaces. By gaining a deeper and more comprehensive understanding of its multifaceted effects and implementing effective strategies for mindful consumption, individuals and teams can effectively harness the power of coffee to significantly boost productivity levels and encourage innovative creativity. Ultimately, fostering a workplace environment that actively promotes healthy coffee habits can lead to improved outcomes for everyone involved, ensuring that coffee serves its purpose as a genuine performance enhancer rather than merely acting as a temporary crutch. By cultivating a vibrant culture that values balance and moderation in coffee consumption, we can maximize the multitude of benefits that coffee offers while minimizing any potential drawbacks that may arise. Through this thoughtful approach, we can create an atmosphere that not only supports individual well-being but also enhances overall team performance.

PART-2

Coffee Break: Revitalize Your Mind for Success

Chapter 1: The Power of a Coffee Break

Understanding the Science of Breaks

Understanding the science of breaks is essential for anyone looking to enhance productivity and mental clarity. Research indicates that taking breaks can significantly improve cognitive function, creativity, and overall performance. Neuroscientists have discovered that short intervals of rest allow the brain to process and consolidate information. During these breaks, the mind can wander, leading to the emergence of new ideas and solutions to problems that may have seemed insurmountable during focused work sessions.

The physiological effects of taking breaks also play a critical role in maintaining mental health. When we engage in prolonged periods of work without interruption, stress levels can rise, leading to burnout and decreased motivation. Breaks trigger a reduction in cortisol, the stress hormone, and promote the release of endorphins, enhancing mood and energy levels. This biological response underscores the importance of incorporating regular breaks into daily routines to sustain long-term productivity and well-being.

Incorporating various types of breaks can further amplify their benefits. Active breaks, such as stretching or taking a brief walk, can invigorate the body and stimulate blood circulation, which in turn enhances brain function.

Conversely, mindfulness breaks, involving practices like meditation or deep breathing, can help calm the mind and sharpen focus. By alternating between these types of breaks, individuals can address both physical and mental fatigue, fostering a more holistic approach to rejuvenation.

The optimal timing and duration of breaks also matter significantly. Research suggests that the most effective breaks typically last between five to fifteen minutes and should occur every hour to maintain peak performance. However, this can vary based on individual preferences and the nature of the tasks at hand. Experimenting with different break schedules can help individuals determine what works best for them, leading to personalized strategies for revitalizing their minds.

Understanding the science of breaks can empower individuals to harness their full potential in both personal and professional pursuits. By acknowledging the physiological and psychological benefits of taking regular breaks, people can cultivate habits that promote sustained productivity and mental clarity. Integrating intentional pauses into daily routines not only aids in preventing burnout but also stimulates creativity, ultimately leading to greater success in various aspects of life.

Historical Perspectives on Coffee and Productivity

The relationship between coffee and productivity has deep historical roots, tracing back to its discovery and subsequent spread across various cultures. Originating in Ethiopia, coffee was initially consumed for its stimulating effects, which were recognized by monks who used it to stay awake during long hours of prayer. As coffee traveled to the Arabian Peninsula, it became a staple in social gatherings and intellectual discourse, fostering an environment where ideas flourished. This early association with alertness and social interaction laid the groundwork for coffee's role in enhancing productivity. By the 17th century, coffee houses emerged as hubs of activity in Europe, particularly in cities like London and Paris. These establishments became known as "penny universities," where patrons could engage in stimulating conversations over a cup of coffee for the price of admission. The coffee house culture nurtured discussions about politics, science, and philosophy, driving progress and innovation. The collective insights generated in these environments highlight how coffee facilitated not just individual productivity, but also collective intellectual advancement, shaping societal development.

As the Industrial Revolution took hold in the 18th and 19th centuries, coffee became increasingly integrated into the daily routines of workers. The beverage was prized for its ability to combat fatigue and enhance focus, allowing laborers to maintain their energy levels during long hours of factory work. Employers began to recognize the value of coffee breaks as a means to boost morale and productivity among workers. This shift represented a significant cultural evolution, as coffee transitioned from a leisure drink to a necessary component of the workday, emphasizing its role in productivity.

In the 20th century, studies began to emerge examining the effects of caffeine on cognitive performance. Research indicated that moderate caffeine consumption could enhance attention, reaction times, and overall cognitive function. This scientific validation of coffee's stimulating effects contributed to its popularity in the workplace. Companies began to implement coffee stations and encourage breaks, recognizing that providing access to coffee could lead to improved employee performance and satisfaction. The understanding of coffee as a productivity tool became increasingly entrenched in corporate culture.

Today, coffee continues to play a vital role in enhancing productivity across various sectors. The modern workplace often includes coffee as a staple in fostering collaboration and creativity among team members. As remote work becomes more prevalent, virtual coffee breaks have emerged as a way to maintain social connections and boost morale. The historical perspectives on coffee and productivity reveal a longstanding recognition of the beverage's potential to energize individuals and stimulate collective progress, making it an enduring ally in the pursuit of success.

Coffee Break: Recharge Your Mind for Peak Performance

The Psychological Benefits of Taking Breaks

Taking breaks is not merely a luxury; it is a necessity for mental well-being and peak performance. In our fast-paced world, where productivity is often prioritized over self-care, the psychological benefits of taking breaks are frequently overlooked. Breaks serve as a powerful tool to rejuvenate the mind, reduce stress, and enhance overall cognitive function. Understanding these benefits can encourage individuals to integrate regular pauses into their routines, ultimately leading to greater success in both personal and professional spheres.

One of the most significant psychological benefits of taking breaks is the reduction of stress levels. Continuous work without rest can lead to mental fatigue, which in turn increases anxiety and stress. When individuals take time away from their tasks, they give their brains a chance to reset. This reset not only alleviates immediate stress but also enables individuals to approach challenges with a clearer mind. Studies have shown that short breaks can lower cortisol levels, the hormone associated with stress, making it easier for individuals to manage their emotions and maintain focus.

Moreover, breaks facilitate improved creativity and problem-solving skills. When people step away from their work, they allow their subconscious to process information in new ways. This period of incubation can lead to innovative ideas and solutions that may not have emerged during focused work sessions. Engaging in activities during breaks, such as going for a walk, practicing mindfulness, or even enjoying a cup of coffee, can stimulate different areas of the brain, fostering a creative mindset. This creative boost can be invaluable in professional settings where fresh ideas are often the key to success.

Additionally, taking breaks helps to enhance focus and productivity in the long run. The brain operates optimally for only a limited amount of time before fatigue sets in. By incorporating regular breaks into work schedules, individuals can maintain higher levels of concentration throughout their tasks.

This practice allows for sustained attention, which is essential for completing complex tasks efficiently. When individuals return from a break, they often find themselves more engaged and motivated, resulting in a productive work session that outpaces those driven solely by prolonged focus.

Finally, breaks contribute to improved emotional well-being. Taking time for oneself, even in short intervals, can lead to feelings of relaxation and contentment. Engaging in enjoyable activities during breaks, whether socializing with colleagues or indulging in a hobby, fosters positive emotions that can counteract the negativity often associated with high-pressure environments. This emotional uplift not only enhances individual morale but can also create a more positive workplace culture, benefiting everyone involved.

In conclusion, the psychological benefits of taking breaks are profound and multifaceted. From reducing stress and enhancing creativity to improving focus and emotional well-being, breaks play a crucial role in maintaining mental health and achieving peak performance. By recognizing the value of these pauses and incorporating them into daily routines, individuals can revitalize their minds and set themselves up for success in their endeavors. Embracing the concept of taking breaks can transform how we work and live, leading to a more balanced and fulfilling existence.

Chapter 2: The Ideal Coffee Break
Timing Your Breaks for Maximum Effect

Timing your breaks effectively is crucial for optimizing mental clarity and productivity throughout the day. Studies have shown that our brains can maintain focus for only a limited period, typically ranging from 25 to 50 minutes, before attention begins to wane. Understanding this natural rhythm can help you schedule your breaks strategically. By taking breaks at the right moments, you can recharge your cognitive resources, leading to improved performance and creativity in your tasks.

One effective method for timing breaks is the **Pomodoro Technique**, which involves working in focused bursts of **25 minutes followed by a 5-minute** break. After four cycles, a longer break **of 15 to 30 minutes** is recommended. This approach not only helps maintain concentration but also creates a structured routine that fosters sustained productivity. During these short breaks, engaging in activities like stretching, deep breathing, or enjoying a quick cup of coffee can significantly enhance your overall mental state, making it easier to return to work with renewed energy.

The type of break you take can also influence its effectiveness. Passive breaks, such as scrolling through social media or watching videos, may not provide the same benefits as active breaks. Engaging in physical activity, whether it's a brief walk or simple exercises, can stimulate blood flow and improve mood. Research indicates that even short bursts of physical movement can lead to increased cognitive function and creativity. Thus, choosing breaks that incorporate movement can be particularly beneficial for maintaining peak performance.

Timing is not just about the length of breaks but also about their frequency. Regularly scheduled breaks throughout the day can prevent burnout and reduce mental fatigue. It's essential to listen to your body and mind; if you find yourself losing focus or feeling overwhelmed, it may be time for a break, even if you're not adhering strictly to your planned schedule. Flexibility allows you to respond to your personal productivity rhythms, ensuring you maximize the effectiveness of your downtime.

Finally, the environment in which you take your breaks can also impact their effectiveness. A change of scenery, such as stepping outside or moving to a different room, can provide a mental reset. Incorporating elements like nature, fresh air, or simply a comfortable space can enhance relaxation and rejuvenation during your breaks. By considering these various factors—timing, type, frequency, and environment—you can tailor your break strategies to not only recharge your mind but also cultivate a more productive and successful work experience.

The Role of Environment in Recharge

The environment plays a crucial role in the process of mental and physical recharge, significantly influencing our capacity to perform at peak levels. Our surroundings, including the physical space we occupy and the sensory experiences we encounter, can either enhance or hinder our ability to rejuvenate. For instance, a cluttered workspace can lead to feelings of stress and distraction, making it difficult to focus and unwind. Conversely, a clean, organized environment promotes clarity and calmness, allowing individuals to recharge effectively. The design and layout of our surroundings are essential factors that can facilitate or obstruct the recharge process.

Natural elements in the environment greatly impact our well-being and mental state. Exposure to nature has been shown to reduce stress, enhance mood, and improve cognitive function. Incorporating green plants, natural light, and outdoor experiences into daily routines can provide significant benefits for mental recharge. For individuals seeking to improve their performance, integrating elements of nature into their workspaces or break areas can create a restorative atmosphere that fosters creativity and productivity. This connection to the natural world is not merely a luxury; it is a necessity for maintaining optimal mental health.

The social environment we find ourselves in also plays a pivotal role in how we recharge. Supportive relationships and positive interactions can uplift our spirits and energize us. Whether through casual conversations with colleagues or spending time with friends, social engagement serves as a crucial buffer against stress. Conversely, negative social interactions or toxic environments can drain energy and reduce motivation. Building a network of supportive individuals and fostering healthy relationships are vital for creating an environment conducive to mental and emotional recharge.

Sound and sensory experiences within our environment are equally important. The presence of soothing sounds, whether from nature or calming music, can enhance relaxation and facilitate a sense of peace. On the other hand, loud, chaotic environments can lead to increased anxiety and decrease our ability to concentrate. Mindfully curating our auditory environment can significantly impact our recharge process. Incorporating practices such as listening to calming music during breaks or utilizing noise-canceling headphones in busy settings can create a more conducive atmosphere for mental recuperation.

Lastly, the overall atmosphere and culture of an environment greatly influence individual recharge. A culture that prioritizes well-being, encourages breaks, and promotes work-life balance creates a supportive space for individuals to rejuvenate. Organizations that recognize the importance of mental health and provide resources for self-care contribute to a positive environment where employees feel valued and empowered. By fostering an atmosphere that encourages recharge, individuals are more likely to thrive and maintain high levels of performance, ultimately leading to greater success in their personal and professional lives.

Choosing the Right Coffee: Types and Their Effects

When selecting the right coffee for your needs, it is essential to understand the various types available, as each type can have different effects on your body and mind. Coffee primarily comes from two beans: Arabica and Robusta. **Arabica** beans are known for their **smooth flavor** and higher acidity, often offering a range of complex tasting notes. In contrast, **Robusta** beans have a **stronger, more bitter** taste and contain more caffeine, making them a popular choice for espresso blends. Understanding these differences can help you choose the right coffee that aligns with your taste preferences and desired effects.

The caffeine content in different types of coffee can significantly affect your energy levels and focus. For instance, espressos, which are made from finely ground coffee beans brewed under high pressure, deliver a concentrated dose of caffeine in a smaller volume. This can provide a quick energy boost, making it ideal for those needing immediate revitalization during a busy workday. On the other hand, a regular brewed coffee allows for a slower release of caffeine, which can sustain energy levels over a more extended period, helping maintain focus during prolonged tasks.

Flavored coffees and specialty blends can also play a role in enhancing your coffee experience. These coffees often incorporate various flavorings, such as vanilla, caramel, or seasonal spices. While they can be enjoyable and provide a delightful sensory experience, it is essential to consider the added sugars and calories in flavored options. For individuals looking to optimize their mental performance, black coffee or lightly brewed coffees may be more beneficial, as they provide the essential caffeine without the potential crash associated with sugar-laden alternatives.

The brewing method you choose can influence not only the flavor but also the health benefits of your coffee. French press coffee, for instance, retains more of the coffee oils, which can enhance flavor but may also raise cholesterol levels if consumed in excess. Conversely, drip coffee makers tend to filter out these oils, producing a cleaner cup. Cold brew coffee, known for its smoothness and lower acidity, can be easier on the stomach and may offer a refreshing option during warmer months. Each brewing method brings unique qualities that can affect overall enjoyment and health impacts. Ultimately, the right coffee for you depends on personal preferences, health considerations, and the effects you seek. Experimenting with different types of coffee, including single-origin varieties, blends, and brewing methods, can lead to discovering what works best for you. Whether you're seeking a quick boost of energy, a moment of relaxation, or sustained focus, understanding the characteristics of various coffees will empower you to make informed choices that enhance your coffee breaks and contribute to your overall success.

Chapter 3: Mindfulness During Your Break
Practicing Mindfulness with Coffee

Practicing mindfulness with coffee is not just about sipping a beverage; it's an opportunity to transform a simple ritual into a powerful tool for mental clarity and focus. Mindfulness, the practice of being present and fully engaged in the moment, can enhance the coffee experience by encouraging individuals to appreciate not only the flavor but also the process of preparation and enjoyment. When approached mindfully, the act of brewing and drinking coffee becomes a meditative practice that can ground and center the mind, making it easier to tackle the tasks of the day.

To begin integrating mindfulness into your coffee routine, start with the preparation process. Choose your favorite coffee beans and take a moment to observe their appearance and aroma. As you grind the beans, focus on the sound and texture, allowing yourself to be fully immersed in the activity. This intentional engagement sets the stage for a mindful experience. The act of brewing coffee can also be seen as a ritual, providing a break from distractions, which is crucial in today's fast-paced world. Embracing this preparation as a sacred time can help establish a calming routine that prepares the mind for the day ahead.

Once your coffee is brewed, take a moment to appreciate its aroma before taking the first sip. This pause allows you to engage your senses fully. Notice the warmth of the cup in your hands and the scent that wafts up to greet you. As you take your first sip, concentrate on the flavors and textures. Is it rich and bold, or light and floral? By focusing on these sensations, you create a deeper connection with the beverage, enhancing not just your enjoyment but also your mindfulness practice. This level of engagement can lead to a greater appreciation of not only coffee but also the present moment.

Mindfulness with coffee extends beyond the act of drinking; it can also serve as a tool for mental clarity throughout the day. For instance, consider taking intentional coffee breaks during work hours. Instead of mindlessly scrolling through your phone or multitasking, dedicate these moments to simply enjoying your coffee. Use this time to reflect on your thoughts, feelings, and the tasks ahead. By doing so, you create a mental reset that can rejuvenate your focus and productivity. These breaks can act as mental checkpoints, reminding you to pause and recalibrate amidst a busy schedule.

Incorporating mindfulness into your coffee routine can lead to a more profound understanding of both your beverage and your state of mind. As you practice this awareness, you may find that it extends beyond coffee into other areas of your life. The ability to be present and fully engaged can enhance your interactions, decision-making, and overall well-being. By embracing coffee as a mindful practice, you not only recharge your mind for peak performance but also cultivate a deeper appreciation for the simple pleasures in life. This holistic approach can transform an everyday habit into a powerful ally in your journey toward success.

Techniques for Focused Breathing

Focused breathing techniques serve as powerful tools to enhance mental clarity and overall well-being, making them essential for anyone looking to revitalize their mind. These techniques can be easily integrated into daily routines, especially during short breaks like those enjoyed with a cup of coffee. By engaging in focused breathing exercises, individuals can reduce stress, improve concentration, and foster a sense of calm, all of which are vital for peak performance.

One effective technique is **diaphragmatic breathing**, often referred to as belly breathing. This method encourages deep inhalation through the nose, allowing the diaphragm to expand fully. As the diaphragm contracts, the abdomen rises while air fills the lungs. This deep breathing technique not only promotes relaxation but also increases oxygen flow to the brain, enhancing cognitive function. Practicing diaphragmatic breathing for a few minutes can significantly lower stress levels and prepare the mind for focused tasks. Another valuable approach is the 4-7-8 breathing technique, which involves inhaling for a count of four, holding the breath for a count of seven, and exhaling for a count of eight. This rhythmic pattern encourages a calm mind and can be particularly beneficial in stressful situations. By extending the exhalation, individuals activate the parasympathetic nervous system, which induces a state of relaxation. This technique can be practiced anytime, making it a perfect fit for the coffee break scenario where quick yet effective methods are needed.

Box breathing is another technique that promotes focus and clarity. It consists of inhaling, holding, exhaling, and holding the breath again, each for a count of four. This structured method helps regulate breath and can be particularly useful during moments of anxiety or overwhelming tasks. Engaging in box breathing during a coffee break can reset the mind and provide a refreshing perspective, allowing for enhanced productivity when returning to work. Lastly, mindful breathing combines focused breathing with mindfulness practices. This technique encourages individuals to pay close attention to their breath, noticing the sensations of inhalation and exhalation without judgment. By anchoring attention to the breath, practitioners can cultivate a present-moment awareness that diminishes distractions and enhances focus. Incorporating mindful breathing into coffee breaks not only revitalizes the mind but also fosters a greater appreciation for the present, leading to improved mental agility and creativity.

Enhancing Creativity through Mindful Moments

In today's fast-paced world, the concept of mindfulness has emerged as a powerful tool for enhancing creativity. Mindful moments, defined as brief periods of focused awareness, can significantly contribute to the generation of new ideas and innovative solutions. By integrating mindfulness practices into daily routines, individuals can cultivate a mental environment conducive to creativity. This subchapter explores various techniques for incorporating mindful moments into your life, demonstrating how even short pauses can lead to enhanced creative thinking.

One effective method for enhancing creativity through mindful moments is the practice of deep breathing. Taking a few minutes to focus on your breath can help clear mental clutter and promote relaxation. As you inhale deeply, visualize the breath filling your mind with clarity and inspiration. Exhaling slowly, imagine releasing any stress or distraction that may hinder your creative process. This simple yet powerful exercise can reset your mental state, allowing fresh ideas to surface more readily.

Another technique is engaging in mindful observation. This involves taking the time to fully immerse yourself in your surroundings, whether you are in a bustling café or a quiet park. By paying attention to the details—the colors, shapes, sounds, and textures—you can stimulate your senses and spark your imagination. Allowing yourself to be present in the moment can lead to unexpected insights and connections that may not have emerged in a more distracted state. Mindful observation encourages a deeper appreciation for the world around you, which can be a rich source of inspiration.

Incorporating creativity-enhancing mindful moments into your daily routine can also be achieved through journaling. Setting aside time to write without judgment can serve as a therapeutic practice that fosters self-expression. During these sessions, focus on your thoughts and feelings, letting them flow freely onto the page. This process not only clears mental blocks but also allows for the exploration of new ideas. Over time, you may find that regular journaling leads to a more profound understanding of your creative impulses and helps you tap into your subconscious mind.

Lastly, incorporating movement into mindful moments can further enhance creativity. Whether through a leisurely walk, yoga, or simple stretching exercises, physical activity can invigorate the mind and body. As you engage in movement, focus on how your body feels and the rhythm of your breath. This awareness can create a sense of flow that encourages innovative thinking. Movement has the potential to break up stagnant thoughts and promote a more dynamic creative process, making it an essential component of mindful practices.

By embracing mindful moments, individuals can unlock new levels of creativity and innovation. The integration of techniques such as deep breathing, mindful observation, journaling, and movement creates a holistic approach to revitalizing the mind. As you commit to these practices, you may discover that your creative potential expands, leading to greater success in both personal and professional endeavors. Mindfulness is not merely a trend; it is a transformative practice that can profoundly enhance creativity and enrich your life.

Chapter 4: The Social Aspect of Coffee Breaks
Building Connections Over Coffee

Building connections over coffee can be a transformative experience, offering more than just a chance to enjoy a warm beverage. When individuals gather around a coffee cup, they create an informal environment conducive to open dialogue and authentic relationship-building. This unique setting allows participants to engage in meaningful conversations, share ideas, and foster a sense of community that can be beneficial both personally and professionally. Coffee breaks serve as an excellent opportunity to network and build connections. The act of sharing a cup of coffee naturally encourages camaraderie, breaking down barriers that may exist in more formal contexts. During these interactions, individuals can discuss their interests, aspirations, and challenges in a relaxed atmosphere. This openness can lead to collaborations, mentorship opportunities, and even friendships that extend beyond the coffee shop.

Moreover, the ritual of meeting for coffee can enhance team dynamics within organizations. Regular coffee breaks can be scheduled to promote collaboration among colleagues, allowing team members to connect on a deeper level. These informal gatherings can lead to increased trust and understanding, ultimately boosting morale and productivity. When employees feel connected to their peers, they are more likely to contribute positively to the work environment, resulting in a more cohesive team.

Building connections over coffee is not limited to workplace interactions; it can also extend to community engagement and personal growth. Local coffee shops often host events that bring together individuals from various backgrounds, creating a melting pot of ideas and experiences. Attending these events can inspire new perspectives, spark creativity, and provide opportunities for personal development. Engaging with diverse groups over coffee can help individuals expand their networks and gain insights that might otherwise be inaccessible.

Ultimately, the act of sharing coffee is a simple yet powerful way to revitalize your mind and enhance your success. By prioritizing these moments of connection, individuals can unlock new possibilities for collaboration, innovation, and growth. The next time you consider taking a break, think of it as an opportunity not just to recharge but also to build meaningful relationships that can enrich your personal and professional life. Embrace the coffee break as a vital tool for connection, and watch as it transforms your approach to networking and collaboration.

The Impact of Social Interaction on Mental Health

Social interaction plays a crucial role in shaping our mental health, influencing our emotional well-being and cognitive function. Engaging with others fosters a sense of belonging and support, which can act as a buffer against stress and anxiety. When individuals connect with friends, family, or colleagues, they often experience an increase in feelings of happiness and self-worth. This positive feedback loop not only enhances mood but also contributes to better problem-solving abilities and creativity, vital components for peak performance in both personal and professional settings.

Research has consistently shown that social connections can reduce the risk of mental health issues. Individuals with strong social networks are less likely to experience depression and anxiety. The presence of friends and family creates a safety net that helps individuals navigate life's challenges. Moreover, social interactions can provide opportunities for individuals to share their experiences and emotions, leading to cathartic conversations. These exchanges can help clarify thoughts and feelings, making it easier to cope with difficult situations.

The quality of social interactions is just as important as the quantity. Meaningful connections with empathetic and understanding individuals can lead to deeper emotional support. Conversely, negative or toxic relationships can contribute to feelings of isolation and stress. Therefore, evaluating the nature of one's social interactions is essential for maintaining mental health. Engaging in positive, supportive environments promotes resilience and encourages personal growth, which is essential for achieving peak performance in any area of life.

In the context of the workplace, social interactions can significantly impact productivity and job satisfaction. Teams that foster collaboration and open communication tend to perform better than those that lack social cohesion. Employees who feel connected to their colleagues are more likely to be engaged and motivated in their roles. This sense of community not only enhances individual performance but also contributes to the overall success of the organization. Building a supportive workplace culture can lead to improved mental health outcomes for employees, ultimately benefiting everyone involved.

To cultivate positive social interactions, individuals can actively seek opportunities to connect with others. This may involve participating in group activities, joining clubs, or simply making an effort to reach out to friends and family regularly. Additionally, incorporating social interactions into daily routines, such as during coffee breaks, can serve as a refreshing mental reset. By prioritizing relationships and fostering a supportive network, individuals can enhance their mental health, paving the way for sustained success and peak performance in all areas of life.

Networking Opportunities in Casual Settings

Networking opportunities often arise in casual settings, providing a unique platform for individuals to connect in a relaxed environment. These informal gatherings, such as coffee breaks, social events, and community meet-ups, can foster genuine relationships that may not materialize in more formal networking scenarios. Engaging in casual conversations over a cup of coffee allows for a comfortable atmosphere where ideas can flow freely and connections can develop organically.

During a coffee break, the pressure to impress is significantly reduced. Participants can share personal stories, experiences, and insights, which can lead to deeper connections. This environment encourages authenticity, allowing individuals to showcase their true selves rather than a polished version that might be typical in a formal networking event. It is within this authenticity that lasting professional relationships can be built, as mutual interests and shared values become clearer.

Casual settings also present opportunities for serendipitous encounters. You never know who might be sitting next to you at a coffee shop or attending a community event. These chance meetings can lead to unexpected collaborations, mentorship opportunities, or even job offers. The key is to remain open and approachable, ready to engage in conversation with anyone who crosses your path. Being receptive to new connections can significantly expand your professional network and open doors that you may not have anticipated.

Moreover, informal networking can enhance creativity and problem-solving. When individuals gather in a relaxed environment, they are often more willing to share ideas and brainstorm solutions without the constraints of a formal agenda. This collaborative spirit can lead to innovative thinking and inspire new approaches to challenges. By leveraging these networking opportunities, individuals can tap into a diverse pool of perspectives, enriching their own understanding and capabilities.

In summary, casual networking settings like coffee breaks are invaluable for fostering meaningful connections and sparking innovative ideas. By

Coffee Break: Recharge Your Mind for Peak Performance

embracing the informality of these occasions, individuals can engage in authentic conversations, encounter unexpected opportunities, and cultivate a network that supports their personal and professional growth. As you navigate your networking journey, remember that sometimes the best connections happen when you least expect them, often over a simple cup of coffee.

Chapter 5: Beyond Coffee: Alternative Breaks

Exploring Herbal Teas and Their Benefits

Herbal teas have gained popularity not only for their diverse flavors but also for their myriad health benefits. Unlike traditional teas that come from the **Camellia** sinensis plant, herbal teas are typically infusions made from a variety of herbs, flowers, fruits, and spices. This broad category allows for a rich variety of options, each offering unique properties that can cater to different needs and preferences. As individuals look for ways to enhance their well-being, herbal teas present an appealing alternative to caffeinated beverages like coffee, providing a moment of relaxation and rejuvenation.

One of the most celebrated benefits of herbal teas is their ability to promote relaxation and reduce stress. **Chamomile tea**, for instance, has long been recognized for its **calming effects** and is often recommended for those struggling with insomnia or anxiety. The gentle sedative properties of chamomile can help soothe the mind, making it easier to unwind after a long day. Similarly, lemon balm and valerian root teas are known for their stress-relieving qualities, providing a natural remedy for those seeking tranquility amidst the chaos of daily life.

In addition to relaxation, numerous herbal teas offer digestive benefits that can enhance overall gut health. **Peppermint tea** is a popular choice for relieving indigestion, bloating, and discomfort. The menthol in peppermint is known to relax the muscles of the gastrointestinal tract, allowing for smoother digestion. Ginger tea, on the other hand, is often used to combat nausea and improve digestion, making it a staple for those who experience digestive issues. Incorporating these herbal teas into one's daily routine can contribute to a healthier digestive system, ultimately supporting better overall health. Herbal teas can also play a significant role in boosting the immune system. Elderberry tea, for example, is renowned for its antiviral properties and is often used to support immune function during cold and flu season. Similarly, echinacea tea has been studied for its potential to reduce the duration and severity of respiratory infections. By including these immune-boosting herbal teas in one's diet, individuals can fortify their defenses against illnesses, which is particularly valuable for those leading busy lives and aiming for peak performance.

Lastly, the antioxidant properties of many herbal teas cannot be overlooked. Rooibos tea, native to South Africa, is rich in antioxidants that help combat oxidative stress in the body. Antioxidants play a crucial role in neutralizing free radicals, which can contribute to chronic diseases and aging. By selecting herbal teas that are high in antioxidants, individuals can enhance their overall health and support long-term wellness. In conclusion, exploring herbal teas offers a wealth of benefits that can enrich one's life, providing opportunities for relaxation, digestive support, immune enhancement, and antioxidant protection, all of which are essential for maintaining peak performance and mental clarity.

Physical Activity as a Revitalizing Break

Physical activity serves as an essential component of a revitalizing break, offering a range of benefits that extend beyond mere physical fitness. Engaging in movement, whether through a brisk walk, stretching, or a quick workout, can significantly enhance mental clarity and focus. During a coffee break, incorporating physical activity allows individuals to step away from the monotony of their tasks and rejuvenate their minds. This shift in focus not only helps to alleviate mental fatigue but also stimulates the brain, preparing it for renewed productivity.

The physiological effects of physical activity are well-documented and contribute to its effectiveness as a revitalizing break. Exercise increases blood circulation, which delivers more oxygen and nutrients to the brain. This enhanced blood flow can lead to improved cognitive functions such as memory, attention, and problem-solving skills. Furthermore, physical activity triggers the release of endorphins, often referred to as "feel-good" hormones, which can elevate mood and reduce stress levels. By incorporating even short bursts of movement, individuals can create a more conducive environment for creativity and innovative thinking.

Incorporating physical activity into coffee breaks doesn't require extensive time or resources. Simple exercises can be performed in various settings, making them accessible to everyone. For instance, desk stretches, short walks around the office, or even a few minutes of light jogging can effectively revitalize the mind. The key is to choose activities that are enjoyable and can easily fit into the break. This not only promotes consistency but also makes the practice of taking a physical break more appealing.

Moreover, the social aspect of physical activity can further enhance its revitalizing effects. Engaging in group activities, such as walking meetings or team-based exercises, fosters a sense of community and collaboration among colleagues. This social interaction can break down barriers, improve communication, and strengthen relationships within the workplace. As a result, these shared experiences not only provide physical benefits but also contribute to a more positive and cohesive work environment.

Ultimately, viewing physical activity as a revitalizing break can lead to a sustainable approach to enhancing both mental and physical well-being. By understanding the profound impact of movement on cognitive function and emotional health, individuals can adopt strategies that prioritize active breaks in their daily routines. This shift in perspective empowers everyone to harness the benefits of physical activity, setting the stage for peak performance, greater productivity, and overall success in their personal and professional lives.

Digital Detox: Reducing Screen Time for a Clear Mind

Digital detox refers to the intentional reduction or complete abstention from digital devices, particularly screens, to regain mental clarity and improve overall well-being. In today's fast-paced world, where smartphones, computers, and tablets dominate our daily routines, the constant bombardment of information can lead to cognitive overload. This subchapter explores the importance of digital detox, its benefits, and practical strategies for minimizing screen time to enhance mental clarity.

One of the primary benefits of reducing screen time is the improvement of focus and concentration. Digital distractions often fragment our attention, making it challenging to engage deeply with tasks or enjoy meaningful conversations. By stepping back from screens, individuals can reclaim their ability to concentrate on one thing at a time, leading to increased productivity and a greater sense of accomplishment. This focused mindset not only enhances work performance but also fosters creativity, allowing for more innovative thinking.

Furthermore, a digital detox can significantly improve mental health. Studies have shown a correlation between excessive screen time and increased levels of anxiety and depression. By disconnecting from social media and news feeds, individuals can alleviate the stress associated with constant comparisons and the pressure to stay updated. This mental break allows for reflection, self-care, and the opportunity to reconnect with hobbies and interests that may have been neglected due to screen overuse.

Implementing a digital detox does not have to be an all-or-nothing approach. Individuals can start by setting specific boundaries for their screen time. For instance, establishing tech-free zones at home, such as during meals or in the bedroom, can encourage more mindful interactions with family and friends. Additionally, designating specific times for checking emails or social media can help create a healthier relationship with technology, ensuring that it serves as a tool rather than a source of stress.

In conclusion, embracing a digital detox is essential in cultivating a clear and focused mind. By recognizing the impact of screen time on mental clarity and well-being, individuals can take proactive steps to reduce digital distractions. The resulting benefits, including improved concentration, enhanced mental health, and meaningful connections with the world around us, can lead to a more balanced and fulfilling life. Taking the time to recharge away from screens is not just a luxury; it is a vital practice for achieving peak performance in both personal and professional endeavors.

Chapter 6: Structuring Your Day for Breaks

The Pomodoro Technique and Its Benefits

The Pomodoro Technique is a time management method developed by Francesco Cirillo in the late 1980s. This technique breaks work into intervals, traditionally 25 minutes in length, separated by short breaks. Each interval is known as a "Pomodoro," named after the Italian word for tomato, inspired by the tomato-shaped kitchen timer Cirillo used during college. The structure of this technique encourages sustained focus and can significantly enhance productivity by allowing individuals to concentrate on a task without the distraction of interruptions.

At the core of the Pomodoro Technique is the idea that the timer creates a sense of urgency. When individuals know they have a limited amount of time to work, they are more likely to stay focused and avoid procrastination. By dedicating 25 minutes to a single task, individuals can dive deep into their work, making substantial progress in a relatively short amount of time. This focused work session is followed by a short break, typically lasting five minutes, which allows the brain to rest and recharge before the next session begins.

One of the key benefits of the Pomodoro Technique is its impact on mental clarity and energy levels. Taking regular breaks helps to prevent burnout and fatigue, which are common challenges in today's fast-paced work environment. During these breaks, individuals can engage in activities that promote relaxation and rejuvenation, such as stretching, grabbing a cup of coffee, or simply stepping away from their workspaces. This balance between intense focus and rest can lead to better overall performance and creativity. Another significant advantage of the Pomodoro Technique is its adaptability to various work styles and tasks. Whether someone is working on a creative project, studying for an exam, or tackling administrative tasks, this method can be tailored to fit individual needs. Users can adjust the length of work intervals and breaks based on their preferences or the nature of the task at hand. This flexibility makes it accessible to a wide range of individuals, ensuring that anyone can implement it into their daily routine.

Lastly, the Pomodoro Technique promotes a sense of accomplishment and motivation. Each completed Pomodoro serves as a mini milestone, providing tangible evidence of progress. Individuals can track their completed sessions and reflect on how much they have achieved throughout the day. This not only boosts morale but also reinforces the habit of focused work. By integrating the Pomodoro Technique into their daily lives, individuals can cultivate a more productive and fulfilling work experience, ultimately leading to greater success in their personal and professional endeavors.

Creating a Balanced Work Schedule

Creating a balanced work schedule is essential for maintaining productivity and ensuring overall well-being. An effective schedule allows individuals to allocate time efficiently for various tasks while also incorporating breaks that are crucial for mental rejuvenation. By prioritizing tasks and establishing a structured routine, one can achieve a harmonious balance between work responsibilities and personal life. This balance not only enhances productivity but also fosters creativity and reduces stress.

To begin crafting a balanced work schedule, it is vital to identify personal priorities and goals. This involves assessing daily tasks and categorizing them based on urgency and importance. Utilizing tools such as to-do lists or digital planners can facilitate this process. By establishing clear objectives for each day, individuals can focus their efforts on what truly matters while avoiding the distraction of less critical tasks. This clarity helps streamline the workday and sets a productive tone from the outset.

Incorporating regular breaks into the work schedule is equally important. Research suggests that taking short, scheduled breaks can significantly improve focus and overall performance. The Pomodoro Technique, for example, encourages individuals to work in intervals, typically 25 minutes, followed by a 5-minute break. This method not only enhances concentration but also provides necessary pauses to recharge mentally. A well-timed coffee break can serve as a perfect opportunity to step away from the desk, allowing the mind to reset and return to tasks with renewed vigor.

Flexibility is another key component of a balanced work schedule. Life is unpredictable, and being rigid with time can lead to unnecessary stress. Allowing for adjustments in the schedule accommodates unforeseen circumstances and personal needs. Whether it's shifting a meeting or rescheduling a project deadline, maintaining a degree of flexibility can help individuals navigate challenges without feeling overwhelmed. This adaptability ensures that one can respond to immediate demands while still keeping long-term goals in sight.

Lastly, it is crucial to regularly evaluate and adjust the work schedule to enhance balance. Periodically reflecting on what is working and what isn't can lead to meaningful changes that optimize productivity. Seeking feedback from peers or using self-assessment tools can provide insights into areas for improvement. By continually refining a work schedule, individuals can ensure it aligns with their evolving personal and professional needs, ultimately leading to a more fulfilling and successful work experience.

Recognizing Signs That You Need a Break

Recognizing when you need a break is essential for maintaining mental clarity and overall well-being. Often, the signs can be subtle, but they manifest in various ways. One of the most common indicators is a persistent sense of fatigue. If you find yourself feeling drained despite a full night's sleep, it may be a signal that your mind needs a rest. Mental fatigue can lead to decreased productivity and increased irritability, making it crucial to listen to your body and mind when they indicate a need for a pause.

Another sign is a decline in focus and concentration. If you notice your thoughts wandering more frequently or struggle to engage with tasks that once held your attention, it could be time to step back. This lack of focus can stem from prolonged periods of work without sufficient breaks, leading to cognitive overload. Taking a break can help reset your focus, allowing for improved concentration when you return to your tasks.

Emotional signs can also indicate the need for a break. Feelings of heightened stress, anxiety, or frustration can emerge when you are pushing yourself too hard. If you find yourself feeling overwhelmed by tasks that previously felt manageable, this emotional strain signals that it might be time to recharge. A short break can provide the necessary space to gain perspective and restore emotional balance, ultimately enhancing your resilience in the face of challenges.

Physical manifestations such as headaches, tension, or changes in appetite can also be indicators that you need to take a step back. These physical symptoms often arise from chronic stress or burnout, which can result from neglecting your need for breaks. Recognizing these signs is crucial; addressing them early can prevent more serious health issues down the line. Taking time to engage in relaxing activities or simply stepping away from your work environment can alleviate these symptoms and promote overall health.

Lastly, consider your motivation levels. A sudden drop in enthusiasm for your work or responsibilities can suggest that you are nearing burnout. When tasks feel like burdens rather than opportunities, it's essential to evaluate your workload and consider taking a break. This time away can reignite your passion and creativity, enabling you to return to your responsibilities with renewed energy and a fresh perspective. Recognizing these signs and responding appropriately can significantly enhance your productivity and

Coffee Break: Recharge Your Mind for Peak Performance

overall quality of life.

Chapter 7: Customizing Your Coffee Break Experience

Personalizing Your Coffee Ritual

Personalizing your coffee ritual can transform a simple daily habit into a revitalizing experience that enhances your mental clarity and overall productivity. The first step in this personalization is to identify the specific qualities of coffee that resonate with you. Consider the flavor profiles you enjoy—do you prefer the rich, bold taste of dark roasts, or the lighter, more complex notes of a medium roast? Exploring various types of beans, such as single-origin varieties or blends, allows you to discover what truly ignites your senses and sets the tone for your day.

Once you have settled on your preferred coffee type, it is essential to establish a brewing method that aligns with your lifestyle and taste. Each brewing technique, whether it's a classic drip coffee maker, a French press, or an espresso machine, imparts different characteristics to the final cup. Experimenting with these methods can reveal surprising nuances in flavor and aroma, helping you to curate a brewing process that feels uniquely yours. Additionally, consider the equipment you use; investing in quality tools can elevate your experience and encourage a sense of pride in your ritual.

Incorporating mindfulness into your coffee preparation can further enhance your experience. Taking a few moments to focus on the process—measuring the beans, grinding them fresh, and watching the coffee bloom—can transform your ritual into a meditative practice. This mindfulness not only enriches your sensory experience but also allows you to be present in the moment, helping to clear your mind of distractions and prepare for the tasks ahead. Setting aside dedicated time for your coffee ritual, free from interruptions, can create a meaningful pause in your day.

Customization extends beyond just the brewing method and ingredients. Consider personalizing your coffee experience with the addition of flavors or enhancements that speak to you. Whether it's a touch of cinnamon, a splash of oat milk, or a hint of vanilla, these additions can enhance the flavor profile of your coffee and make each cup a unique reflection of your tastes. Furthermore, utilizing seasonal ingredients or local specialties can infuse a sense of adventure and novelty into your ritual, keeping it fresh and exciting. Finally, the environment in which you enjoy your coffee plays a crucial role in personalizing your ritual. Creating a dedicated coffee nook or a cozy corner can provide a sanctuary for your moments of peace and reflection. Surround yourself with items that inspire you, such as books, artwork, or even plants. The ambiance of your coffee space can significantly influence your mood and mindset, contributing to a more fulfilling coffee break that revitalizes your mind for peak performance. As you cultivate this personalized experience, you will find that your coffee ritual becomes an essential part of your daily routine, equipping you with the mental clarity needed to tackle your goals.

Incorporating Snacks for Nutritional Boost

Incorporating snacks into your daily routine can significantly enhance your overall nutrition and energy levels. For individuals seeking to revitalize their minds and maintain peak performance, understanding the role of snacks is essential. Healthy snacking provides the body with the necessary fuel to manage stress, sustain focus, and enhance cognitive function. By selecting the right snacks, you can transform your coffee breaks into opportunities for nourishing both your body and mind.

When choosing snacks, it is crucial to prioritize nutrient-dense options that provide sustained energy rather than quick fixes that may lead to energy crashes. Foods rich in complex carbohydrates, healthy fats, and proteins will help maintain stable blood sugar levels, which is vital for prolonged concentration and productivity. For instance, whole grain crackers with hummus or a handful of nuts can provide the necessary macronutrients to keep you alert and focused during your workday.

In addition to macronutrients, incorporating a variety of vitamins and minerals through your snacks can further enhance cognitive function. Fruits such as berries, bananas, and apples are excellent choices, as they are packed with antioxidants and vitamins that support brain health. Dark chocolate is another option that, in moderation, can provide a quick energy boost while improving mood and cognitive performance due to its high flavonoid content. By diversifying your snack choices, you ensure that your body receives a broad spectrum of nutrients essential for optimal brain function.

Planning your snacks ahead of time can help you make healthier choices and avoid reaching for less nutritious options when hunger strikes. Preparing snack packs with pre-cut vegetables, yogurt, or homemade energy bars can streamline your snacking process, making it easier to stay on track with your nutritional goals. Keeping these healthy snacks readily available during your coffee breaks can also serve as a reminder to prioritize your well-being amidst a busy day.

Ultimately, the incorporation of snacks into your daily routine is not merely about staving off hunger; it is about consciously fueling your body and mind for success. By selecting nutrient-rich snacks and planning ahead, you can enhance your cognitive performance, improve your mood, and maintain the energy necessary to tackle challenges effectively. Embracing the habit of mindful snacking can lead to lasting benefits that contribute to both personal and professional achievements.

Experimenting with Different Coffee Break Activities

Experimenting with different coffee break activities can significantly enhance the benefits of taking short, intentional breaks throughout the day. Traditional coffee breaks often revolve around simply consuming coffee and chatting with colleagues. However, diversifying these activities can lead to increased creativity, improved focus, and enhanced team dynamics. By integrating various activities into your coffee breaks, you can revitalize your mind and promote a more productive work environment.

One effective approach is to incorporate physical movement into your coffee break routine. Engaging in light stretching or a short walk can stimulate circulation and boost energy levels. This physical activity not only recharges the body but also clears the mind, allowing for renewed focus upon returning to work tasks. Simple exercises, such as desk stretches or brief yoga routines, can be done in the office or nearby outdoor spaces, making them accessible and easy to implement.

Another innovative option is to introduce mindfulness practices during coffee breaks. Mindfulness techniques, such as meditation or deep breathing exercises, can help reduce stress and enhance mental clarity. Taking just a few minutes to practice mindfulness can create a sense of calm and improve overall well-being. Organizations can facilitate this by providing resources, such as guided meditation apps or even hosting short sessions led by trained professionals.

Creative activities can also serve as a refreshing alternative to the standard coffee break. Engaging in artistic pursuits, such as doodling, coloring, or writing, allows individuals to express themselves and tap into their creative potential. These activities can foster a sense of playfulness and encourage innovative thinking. Setting up a communal art station or organizing themed creative challenges during breaks can promote collaboration and camaraderie among team members.

Finally, incorporating educational elements into coffee breaks can enrich the experience. Hosting short presentations, discussion groups, or book clubs can stimulate intellectual engagement and foster a culture of continuous learning. These activities not only make breaks more meaningful but also provide opportunities for personal and professional development. By experimenting with various coffee break activities, individuals and teams can discover what resonates most, ultimately leading to a more energized and productive work environment.

Chapter 8: Overcoming Barriers to Taking Breaks
Addressing Workplace Culture and Expectations

Addressing workplace culture and expectations is crucial for fostering an environment where individuals can thrive and achieve peak performance. The culture within an organization encompasses shared values, beliefs, and behaviors that shape how employees interact with one another and approach their work. Establishing a positive workplace culture encourages collaboration, innovation, and accountability, which ultimately leads to improved productivity and job satisfaction. Organizations must actively cultivate a culture that aligns with their mission and values, ensuring that every employee feels included and valued.

One key aspect of workplace culture is the clear communication of expectations. Employees need to understand what is required of them to excel in their roles. This includes not only job responsibilities but also behavioral expectations that influence team dynamics. Leaders should provide regular feedback, set measurable goals, and create an open dialogue where employees feel comfortable discussing challenges and seeking guidance. When expectations are transparent, employees are more likely to align their efforts with organizational objectives, fostering a sense of purpose and direction. Another important factor in shaping workplace culture is the emphasis on inclusivity and diversity. A diverse workforce brings a wealth of perspectives and ideas, which can enhance creativity and problem-solving. Organizations should prioritize inclusivity by implementing policies and practices that promote equity and respect for all employees. This can involve providing diversity training, creating employee resource groups, and actively seeking input from individuals at all levels. By embracing diversity, companies not only improve their workplace culture but also position themselves for greater success in a global market.

Recognition and appreciation play a vital role in reinforcing a positive workplace culture. Employees who feel recognized for their contributions are more engaged and motivated to perform at their best. Organizations should establish regular recognition programs that celebrate both individual and team achievements. This could be as simple as shout-outs in meetings or more formal awards and incentives. By acknowledging the hard work and accomplishments of employees, organizations foster a sense of belonging and loyalty that can enhance overall morale and productivity.

Finally, organizations must be adaptable and responsive to the evolving needs of their employees. Workplace culture is not static; it requires ongoing assessment and refinement. Leaders should solicit feedback from employees through surveys, focus groups, or informal conversations to understand their experiences and expectations. This feedback can inform adjustments to policies, practices, and the overall work environment. By demonstrating a commitment to continuous improvement and responsiveness to employee needs, organizations can create a thriving workplace culture that supports peak performance and long-term success.

Time Management Strategies for Busy Schedules

Effective time management is essential for anyone navigating a busy schedule. With numerous responsibilities vying for attention, it can be easy to feel overwhelmed. The first strategy to consider is prioritization. This involves identifying the most critical tasks that require immediate attention versus those that can wait. Utilizing tools like the **Eisenhower Matrix** can help distinguish between urgent and important tasks, allowing individuals to focus their efforts on what truly matters. By regularly assessing priorities, one can ensure that time is spent on activities that align with both personal and professional goals.

Another key time management strategy is the implementation of time blocks. This technique involves allocating specific periods for different tasks or activities throughout the day. By setting aside dedicated time for work, meetings, and even breaks, individuals can create a structured routine that minimizes distractions and enhances productivity. For instance, designating the first hour of the day for deep work can lead to significant progress on important projects. Additionally, incorporating short breaks within these blocks can rejuvenate the mind, providing the necessary refreshment needed to maintain focus.

Incorporating technology into time management can also yield significant benefits. Various applications and tools are available that assist in scheduling, tracking tasks, and setting reminders. Tools like digital calendars or project management software can streamline the process, making it easier to visualize deadlines and commitments. By leveraging these resources, individuals can reduce the mental load associated with remembering every task and instead focus on execution. This not only increases efficiency but also frees up mental space for creativity and strategic thinking.

Delegation is another effective strategy for managing time, particularly for those in leadership or collaborative roles. Understanding that one cannot do everything alone is crucial. By identifying tasks that can be delegated to team members or colleagues, individuals can redistribute their workload, allowing them to concentrate on higher-priority activities. This fosters a sense of teamwork and can also enhance the skills and capabilities of those involved, creating a more productive work environment for everyone.

Lastly, regular reflection and adjustment of time management strategies are vital for ongoing success. As schedules and priorities change, it is essential to evaluate what is working and what is not. Setting aside time each week to review accomplishments and challenges can provide valuable insights into productivity patterns. This allows for the fine-tuning of approaches to time management, ensuring that they remain effective in the face of evolving demands. By continuously adapting strategies, individuals can maintain control over their schedules and ultimately achieve their professional and personal aspirations.

Combatting Guilt Associated with Taking Breaks

Taking breaks is often viewed through a lens of guilt, particularly in high-pressure environments where productivity is heavily emphasized. Many individuals struggle with the notion that pausing for a moment to recharge may somehow equate to laziness or lack of dedication. This mindset not only undermines the benefits of taking breaks but can also lead to burnout, decreased productivity, and overall dissatisfaction with work. Recognizing and addressing these feelings of guilt is crucial for fostering a healthier relationship with work and improving overall performance.

Understanding the psychological and physiological benefits of breaks can help alleviate guilt. Research has shown that taking regular breaks enhances cognitive function, boosts creativity, and improves mood. When individuals allow themselves the time to step away, even briefly, they often return to their tasks with renewed focus and energy. This rejuvenation can lead to higher quality work and more efficient use of time, ultimately benefiting both the individual and the organization. Acknowledging these advantages can help shift the narrative around breaks from one of guilt to one of necessity.

To combat the guilt associated with taking breaks, it is essential to reframe the perception of productivity. Instead of equating constant busyness with effectiveness, individuals should recognize that true productivity encompasses not only output but also the quality of work. Emphasizing the importance of mental well-being and recognizing that breaks are a key component of maintaining high performance can foster a more positive view of downtime. Encouraging a culture where breaks are normalized and even celebrated can also play a significant role in reducing feelings of guilt.

Developing a structured approach to breaks may further mitigate feelings of guilt. Implementing scheduled coffee breaks or short periods of relaxation can create a sense of routine and purpose. By allocating specific times for breaks, individuals can mentally prepare for these intervals, allowing them to enjoy the time off without the nagging worry of unfinished tasks. This structured approach not only helps in planning workload but also reinforces the idea that breaks are an integral part of a productive day rather than an interruption. Lastly, self-compassion is a vital tool in overcoming guilt associated with taking breaks. Individuals should remind themselves that everyone deserves time to recharge, and it is not a reflection of their work ethic or capabilities. Practicing self-kindness and understanding that taking breaks is a universal necessity can empower individuals to embrace this practice without shame. By fostering a mindset of self-compassion, individuals can cultivate a healthier, more balanced approach to work that prioritizes both productivity and well-being.

Chapter 9: Success Stories: Coffee Breaks in Action
Case Studies from Various Industries

In examining the impact of short breaks on productivity, various industries provide compelling case studies that illustrate the benefits of taking time to recharge. One notable example comes from the tech industry, where companies like **Google and Microsoft have incorporated break areas** and relaxation zones into their office designs. These spaces encourage employees to step away from their desks, engage in casual conversations, or simply enjoy a moment of solitude. Research indicates that these brief interludes help reset cognitive functions, ultimately leading to enhanced creativity and problem-solving abilities. Employees return to their tasks with fresh perspectives, demonstrating how structured breaks can significantly increase overall efficiency.

In the healthcare sector, studies have shown that medical professionals who take scheduled breaks exhibit lower levels of fatigue and burnout. **Hospitals** that implement mandatory downtime during shifts report higher job satisfaction among staff, which translates into better patient care. For instance, a hospital in **New York City** introduced a program that required nurses to take at least a 15-minute break every few hours. The results were striking; not only did nurse well-being improve, but patient outcomes also showed marked enhancements. This case exemplifies how prioritizing mental health in high-stress environments can lead to substantial performance gains. The education sector also benefits from the practice of taking short breaks.

Schools that have adopted the **'Brain Breaks' concept**, which involves brief physical activities or mindfulness exercises during class, report improved student focus and engagement. A middle school in California implemented a structured break system where students participate in five-minute activities that vary from stretching to mindfulness practices. Teachers noted that students returned to their lessons more alert and ready to learn, which contributed to better academic performance. This case highlights the importance of mental rejuvenation in learning environments and its role in fostering a conducive atmosphere for education.

The hospitality industry provides another insightful example of the effectiveness of coffee breaks and downtime. A well-known hotel chain initiated a program that encouraged staff to take regular breaks throughout their shifts. These breaks were designed not only for relaxation but also for staff to share experiences and insights with one another. As a result, employee morale improved alongside service quality, leading to increased guest satisfaction. The case shows that fostering a culture of well-being among employees can directly influence customer experiences and drive business success.

Lastly, the manufacturing sector has recognized the value of regular breaks in enhancing productivity and safety. A leading automotive manufacturer implemented a policy that mandated breaks every two hours for assembly line workers. This change resulted in a significant decrease in workplace accidents and an increase in output. Workers reported feeling more energized and focused, which contributed to higher overall efficiency. The case study serves as a powerful testament to the idea that prioritizing rest and recovery can lead to both improved employee welfare and enhanced operational performance.

Testimonials from High Performers

Testimonials from high performers offer valuable insights into the practices and mindsets that contribute to success. Many individuals in various fields have discovered that integrating mindful breaks into their routines can significantly enhance their productivity and creativity. These testimonials serve not only as inspiration but also as practical examples of how a simple coffee break can lead to profound results in both personal and professional spheres. One prominent entrepreneur shared her experience of incorporating coffee breaks into her daily schedule. She noted that these pauses not only provided a moment of respite but also served as a catalyst for her most innovative ideas. By stepping away from her desk, she allowed her mind to wander freely, leading to breakthroughs that she might not have achieved while entrenched in work. Her testimony emphasizes the importance of giving oneself permission to take a break, arguing that this practice fosters a healthier work environment and ultimately drives success.

A renowned athlete also testified to the power of mindful breaks. He described how, during intense training periods, he relied on short coffee breaks to refocus his energy and sharpen his mental game. These intervals were not merely about caffeine intake; they became ritualistic moments where he could reflect on his goals and visualize his performance. His perspective highlights that revitalizing the mind is just as crucial as physical training, asserting that mental clarity can be a game-changer when faced with competitive challenges.

In the academic world, a professor shared how he encourages his students to take coffee breaks during study sessions. He has observed that these breaks lead to enhanced retention and understanding of complex material. By stepping away from their books, students return with renewed focus and a clearer perspective. This approach has transformed his teaching methodology, demonstrating that strategic breaks can significantly impact learning outcomes and academic performance.

Lastly, a tech industry leader spoke about the culture of innovation within his company, attributing much of its success to the practice of regular coffee breaks. He emphasized that these moments of downtime foster collaboration and idea-sharing among team members. By creating an environment where employees feel comfortable taking breaks together, he has seen an increase in creativity and team cohesion. His testimony reinforces the notion that a simple coffee break can serve as a powerful tool for enhancing teamwork and driving organizational success.

Lessons Learned from Successful Break Practices

Successful break practices are essential for enhancing productivity and mental clarity, offering valuable lessons that can be applied in various aspects of life. One of the primary lessons learned is the importance of intentionality in taking breaks. Rather than allowing breaks to become mindless distractions, effective practices emphasize the need to plan and purposefully engage in activities that recharge the mind. This intentional approach ensures that breaks serve their intended purpose, allowing individuals to return to their tasks with renewed focus and energy.

Another key lesson is the significance of variety in break activities. Engaging in different types of breaks can prevent monotony and keep the mind stimulated. Successful break practices often incorporate activities that vary in nature, such as physical exercise, mindfulness meditation, or creative pursuits. This diversity caters to different preferences and needs, enabling individuals to discover what works best for them. By experimenting with various break activities, one can identify the most effective ways to rejuvenate and inspire creativity.

The role of the environment during breaks also plays a crucial part in their success. A conducive environment can greatly enhance the effectiveness of break practices. Successful individuals often seek out spaces that promote relaxation and mental clarity, whether through natural light, comfortable seating, or calming surroundings. By creating a dedicated space for breaks, people can cultivate a habit of stepping away from work while signaling their brain that it's time to recharge. This shift in environment helps to create a clear boundary between work and rest, enhancing overall productivity.

Incorporating social interactions during breaks can further amplify their benefits. Engaging with colleagues or friends during these moments can foster a sense of community and support, which is essential for mental well-being. Successful break practices often highlight the importance of connecting with others, as these social interactions can lead to the exchange of ideas and a boost in morale. The lessons learned from these practices emphasize that taking breaks with others can transform a solitary experience into a collaborative one, ultimately enhancing creativity and problem-solving. Lastly, consistency is a vital lesson derived from successful break practices. Regularly scheduled breaks can create a rhythm that enhances overall productivity. Those who have mastered the art of break-taking often integrate this practice into their daily routines, ensuring that they prioritize their mental health alongside their work responsibilities. By establishing a habit of taking intentional breaks, individuals can maintain peak performance over time, leading to sustained success and a healthier work-life balance.

Chapter 10: Creating a Coffee Break Plan
Setting Goals for Your Breaks

Setting goals for your breaks can significantly enhance the effectiveness of your downtime, especially in the context of a busy work environment. Breaks are often viewed as mere pauses in productivity, but with intentional goal setting, they can become powerful tools for rejuvenation and focus. By establishing clear objectives for your breaks, you can maximize their potential to recharge your mind and prepare you for the tasks ahead.

One effective approach to setting goals for your breaks is to consider what you genuinely need at that moment. This might entail physical rest, mental relaxation, or even social interaction. By reflecting on your current state—whether you feel fatigued, stressed, or creatively blocked—you can tailor your break activities to meet those needs. For instance, if you are mentally drained, a quiet moment with a cup of coffee in solitude may be ideal. Conversely, if you feel isolated, connecting with a colleague for a brief chat could provide the social boost necessary to invigorate your spirit.

Another important aspect of goal setting during breaks is to integrate activities that promote mindfulness and presence. Engaging in practices such as deep breathing, meditation, or simply taking a walk can help you clear your mind and reduce stress. Setting a goal to engage in a mindfulness exercise during each break can create a routine that fosters mental clarity and emotional stability. This intentional approach not only enhances the quality of your breaks but also cultivates a habit of returning to your work with renewed focus and creativity.

Additionally, consider incorporating short, achievable goals that align with your long-term objectives. For example, if your overarching aim is to improve your physical health, a break could include a quick stretch or a few minutes of light exercise. Alternatively, if you are working on personal development, you might set a goal to read a few pages of a motivational book or listen to a podcast. These small, goal-oriented activities can transform your breaks into valuable opportunities for growth and self-improvement, rather than just moments of idle time.

Finally, regularly reassess your break goals to ensure they remain relevant and effective. As your workload and personal circumstances change, so too should your break strategies. Make it a habit to evaluate the impact of your breaks on your overall productivity and well-being. By adjusting your goals based on what you learn about your needs and preferences, you can continue to refine your break practices, making them an integral part of your journey toward peak performance and success.

Tracking Your Progress and Adjusting

Tracking your progress is a crucial element in achieving any goal, whether personal or professional. By consistently monitoring your advancements, you can identify what strategies work best for you and which areas may require adjustments. This process not only keeps you accountable but also motivates you as you witness the tangible results of your efforts. Simple tools such as journals, progress charts, or mobile applications can facilitate this tracking, making it easier to visualize your journey and celebrate milestones along the way.

Incorporating regular check-ins into your routine is essential for effective progress tracking. Set aside specific times to review your goals and evaluate your performance. This could be weekly, monthly, or even quarterly, depending on the nature of your objectives. During these check-ins, assess not only what you have accomplished but also the obstacles you encountered.

Understanding the reasons behind any setbacks can provide valuable insights that will inform your future actions and help you stay aligned with your goals. Adjusting your strategies based on your progress is equally important. As you track your performance, you may discover that certain approaches yield better results than others. Being flexible and open to change allows you to refine your methods and enhance your efficiency over time. This adaptability is particularly beneficial in environments that are constantly evolving, as it enables you to remain relevant and competitive. Embrace the idea that adjustments are not failures but rather opportunities for growth and improvement.

Moreover, it is essential to celebrate your successes, regardless of how small they may seem. Recognizing your achievements boosts your motivation and reinforces positive behavior. Create a system of rewards for yourself as you reach specific milestones. This could be as simple as taking a short coffee break to enjoy your favorite brew or treating yourself to a well-deserved day off. These rewards not only provide a moment of joy but also serve as a reminder of your hard work and dedication.

Finally, remember that tracking progress and making adjustments is an ongoing process. Success is rarely linear, and setbacks can occur at any stage of your journey. Embrace the idea that your path may twist and turn, and remain committed to adapting your strategies as needed. By fostering a mindset that values reflection and continual improvement, you set yourself up for sustained success. In doing so, you ensure that you are not just moving forward but advancing with purpose and clarity, ultimately revitalizing your mind for peak performance.

Building a Sustainable Coffee Break Habit

Incorporating a sustainable coffee break habit into your daily routine can significantly enhance your mental clarity and overall productivity. A coffee break is not merely a pause from work; it serves as a vital opportunity to recharge and refocus. To build this habit effectively, it is essential to establish a consistent schedule that aligns with your work rhythm. Identify specific times during the day when you feel your energy waning, and plan your coffee breaks accordingly. This intentionality helps create a structured routine, making it easier to integrate these pauses into your day.

Choosing the right environment for your coffee breaks can also contribute to their sustainability. Consider finding a cozy spot away from your usual work area, whether that's a quiet corner of your office, a nearby café, or even an outdoor space. A change of scenery can stimulate your creativity and refresh your perspective. Additionally, ensure that your break area is comfortable and inviting, with adequate seating and minimal distractions. This environment will encourage you to take the time you need to unwind and recharge, promoting a more effective break.

Mindfulness plays a crucial role in making your coffee breaks truly restorative. Instead of mindlessly scrolling through your phone or catching up on emails, use this time to engage in activities that foster relaxation and mental clarity. Savor your coffee, focusing on its aroma and flavor, or take a few moments to practice deep breathing or meditation. These practices can help clear your mind and reduce stress, allowing you to return to your tasks with renewed energy and focus. Consider incorporating short stretches or light physical activity during your break to further enhance your mental and physical well-being.

Another aspect of a sustainable coffee break habit is social interaction. Connecting with colleagues or friends during your breaks can enhance your mood and strengthen relationships. Engaging in light conversation can provide a refreshing mental shift, making your break more enjoyable and fulfilling. However, it's essential to strike a balance; while socializing can be beneficial, be mindful of the time spent on these interactions to ensure you return to work feeling refreshed rather than overwhelmed.

Finally, reflect on your coffee break routine regularly to assess its effectiveness. Determine which elements are working well and which may need adjustment. Gathering feedback from peers or journaling about your experiences can provide valuable insights into how your breaks influence your productivity and overall well-being. By continually refining your coffee break habit, you can ensure that it remains a sustainable and beneficial part of your daily routine, ultimately contributing to your success and peak performance.

Author

Gerald S. Carolino, BSc, RMEE, ASEAN Engr, LEED GA, MBA, MPM, is a seasoned engineer and writer with years of experience in the construction industry. A dedicated professional, Gerald holds a Master's Degree in Project Management and an MBA from Isabel Universidad in Spain. He earned his Bachelor of Science in Mechanical Engineering from Adamson University. As an ISO 9001:2015 Certified Professional and LEED Green Associate, Gerald is also a Registered ASEAN Engineer. His career reflects leadership and expertise, having served two years on the PSME Board of Directors. When not immersed in his professional work, Gerald enjoys the simple pleasure of a good cup of coffee, often savouring it while reflecting on ideas or unwinding at home in New Jersey or a bustling street in New York. Beyond his work and personal interests, he is a devoted husband and father, driven by his motto, **"Never Give Up."**

"At home in New Jersey, USA, with the coffee machine and coffee."

www.ingramcontent.com/pod-product-compliance
Lightning Source LLC
Chambersburg PA
CBHW070158230526
45471CB00002B/718